Amit Joshi
New York
27 April 1991

Everything You Ever Wanted to Know

KISSING

tomima edmark

A Fireside Book

PUBLISHED BY SIMON & SCHUSTER INC. ❤ NEW YORK LONDON TORONTO SYDNEY TOKYO SINGAPORE

FIRESIDE
Simon & Schuster Building
Rockefeller Center
1230 Avenue of the Americas
New York, New York 10020

Text Copyright © 1991 by Tomima Edmark
Illustrations Copyright © 1991 by Kevin Bapp

FIRESIDE and colophon are registered trademarks
of Simon & Schuster Inc.

DESIGNED BY BONNI LEON
Manufactured in the United States of America

10   9   8   7   6   5   4   3   2   1

Library of Congress Cataloging in Publication Data
Edmark, Tomima.
    Kissing: everything you ever wanted to know/by Tomima Edmark.
        p.   cm.
    Summary: A complete guide to kissing with a brief history, quotes, facts and
trivia, detailed instructions, and expert advice.
    1. Kissing—Juvenile literature.   [1. Kissing.]   I. Title.
GT2640.E36   1991
394—dc20   90-49404
                                                                    CIP
                                                                    AC

ISBN 0-671-70883-X

contents

Two teachers
touched my life,
changing it forever.
This book is dedicated
to the memory of
Helena Stawski
&
Elsa Chinn

introduction

Since the early sixties, we've been bombarded with how-to books on sexual intercourse to the point that we suffer from information overload. Yet kissing, which provides our first physical expression of affection, has been examined only in private.

Is it that kissing is so simple that it needs no investigation? Any woman who has walked away from a kiss with a stubble burn or any man who has had his ear drenched will beg to differ. There are most definitely correct and incorrect ways to kiss.

What woman, for example, hasn't sacrificed the basic body function of breathing to a partner who gave little thought to smashing her nose up against his face. (No, that gasp probably wasn't in ecstasy, but for air!) Then there are the slobberers who leave your face feeling as if it's been slimed Ghostbusters-style. With dogs, the habit is endearing; with humans, it's repulsive. Power kissers, who smooch under the delusion that the harder it is the better, shouldn't be overlooked, either. And, of course, there are those whose idea of a successful "French kiss" means tackling your uvula with their tongue. I could go on and on, but here's the point: there's much to be learned about this kissing business.

Kissing will help you avoid many of the kissing pitfalls and will elevate your kissing skills regardless of your current expertise. For first-time kissers, a sure-fire kissing approach is blocked out, with step-by-step instructions to reduce your anxiety over that initial romantic kiss and make its experience a successful and memorable one. Most experienced kissers can expand their kissing repertoire with an extensive list of kisses and embraces with explicit, illustrated directions. Kissers in long-standing relationships will find a section on how to take the kissing technique to an extraordinary level, and perhaps rekindle a romantic fire.

"Prelude to a Kiss" will not only help you in future Trivial Pursuit games but give you some enlightening information on this enjoyable activity. "Kissing Basics" furnishes the essentials of what you need to know about the act of kissing. Think of this as the "How To" section. Finally, "Mastering the Art" builds on all the previous chapters to present you with a variety of new ways to enhance your kissing style even if you're already a knowledgeable kisser. I encourage you folks especially to peruse the entire book.

No law or faith restricts the act of kissing to only those who are married. It's the inalienable right of every man, woman, and child to kiss. With this in mind, I hope this book establishes two facts: kissing is one of the most intimate forms of human contact, *and* it is a very important step in romance. No longer should kissing be regarded merely as a warm-up to whoopee; kissing should be given the time and attention it deserves. And, at last, I hope this book will increase the kissing talent out there. Let's eradicate poor puckering in our lifetime. With that, I hope you enjoy this book.

prelude
to a kiss

♥

A KISS IS JUST A KISS—
BUT WHAT'S A KISS?

♥

What is a kiss? This simple and straightforward question has no easy answer. The *Webster's New Collegiate Dictionary* defines the verb "to kiss" as "to touch with the lips. . . ." This definition captures the basic action of a kiss perhaps, but it certainly falls short of a comprehensive explanation. Really, wouldn't you be disappointed to learn that the romantic kiss you just experienced was merely lip grazing? A kiss has emotion, meaning, and gesture. But what is a kiss?

Some people have taken
a rather pragmatic approach
to explain the kiss:

"The anatomical juxtaposition of two orbicularis oris muscles in a state of contraction."
    Dr. Henry Gibbons, "Definition of a Kiss"

"A kiss is produced by a kind of sucking movement of the muscles of the lips, accompanied by a weaker or louder sound. It must be in contact with a creature or object, otherwise you could be calling a horse."
    Christopher Nyrop

"A pressure of the mouth against the body."
Dictionary of the Danish Philological Society

"A bite and a suction."
P. d'Enjoy

"An interchange of labial microbes."
Santiage y Cajalc

"A vigorous exchange of saliva."
Anonymous

Others are struck by a kiss's sentiment. Their depiction of a kiss has taken a passionate and poetic angle:

"What is a kisse? Why this, as some approve;
The sure sweet cement, glue and lime of love."
Robert Herrick, *"A Kiss,"* Hesperides *(1648)*

"Four sweet lips, two pure souls, and one undying affection—
these are love's pretty ingredients for a kiss."
Christian Nestell Bovee

"A word invented by the poets to rhyme with 'bliss.' "
Ambrose Bierce

"To a young girl, faith; to a married woman, hope; to an old maid, charity."
V. P. Skipper

"The blossom of love."
    Ancient Greek poet

"Kisses are like grains of gold or silver found upon the ground, of no value themselves, but precious as showing that a mine is near."
    George Villiers

"Love's lesser lightning."
    Sir John Suckling

"I am just two and two, I am warm, I am cold,
And the parents of numbers that cannot be told,
I am lawful, unlawful—a duty, a fault—
I am often sold dear, good for nothing when bought;
An extraordinary boon, and a matter of course,
And yielded with pleasure when taken by force."
    William Cowper

Of course, humor can be found in any circumstance. Kissing is no exception. Several witty observations are duly noted:

"A kiss sounds the same as when a cow drags her hind hoof out of a swamp."
    Old German metaphor

"Lip service to love."
    Warren Golderg

"A pleasant reminder that two heads are better than one."
            Rex Prauty

"Something that often leads to marriage because it leaves something to be desired."
            Definition adapted from Robert Fontaine

"At twenty, a kiss is an experiment,
at forty a sentiment,
and after that a compliment."
            Anonymous

"A thing of use to no one, but prized by two."
            Robert Zwickey

"The kiss is a wordless articulation of desire whose object lies in the future, and somewhat to the south."
            Lance Morrow

"A contraction of the mouth due to an enlargement of the heart."
            Anonymous

"A kiss is a lovely trick designed by nature to stop speech when words become superfluous."
            Ingrid Bergman

These interpretations encompass a wide range of kissing revelations from the practical to the passionate. The famous writer Elizabeth Meriwether Gilmer (alias Dorothy Dix) was obviously gastronomically inspired when she commented that "Nobody wants to kiss when they are hungry." This assortment of kissing commentaries proves only that a kiss is not easily defined.

The phenomenon of kissing plays a very important role throughout your life. For a child, kissing symbolizes love and approval, is a reward for being good, and is a warm send-off to a good night's sleep. Mom's kisses have magical powers to make the hurt go away. Kissing can even break spells to awaken Sleeping Beauties and turn frogs into princes. So from the start, kissing is a very pleasurable concept.

In adolescence, kissing becomes more complicated with the transition from innocence to romance. You find yourself pressured to perform your first romantic kiss before your sixteenth birthday. You can no longer be kissed by just *anyone*. Kissing turns into a very serious matter. You discover "kissing anxiety."

Later in life, the kiss marks your first step to love-play and all its physical aspects. It seals your marriage vows. Then kissing comes full circle and once again serves as an accepted greeting by friends and family, and a symbol of love and approval.

Because the kiss is so simple in design and easy to perform, we have found other uses for it in addition to those that mark the milestones through life. We kiss to say hello or good-bye. We kiss for luck or for sympathy. We seal things with a kiss. We celebrate with a kiss. We sometimes kiss the ground others walk on. Politicians kiss babies. Men and boys steal kisses; women and girls usually let them. We avoid kissing and telling. We encourage kissing to make up. We try to avoid the Judas kiss, the kiss of death, and kissing the porcelain god. And eventually, we all kiss the dust.

A kiss is the most intimate form of contact between a man and a woman. The mouth and lips are androgynous, allowing partners to communicate as biological equals, so kissing can be considered common ground between the sexes. Unlike any other sensual act, kissing makes each partner aware of what the other is feeling.

The mucous membranes of the lips are the most easily accessible of the body's erogenous zones, and perhaps the most important. In fact, the sector of the brain that deals with messages from the lips is bigger than that which handles impulses from the entire torso. The lips hold tremendous potential to please.

With this symmetry and proximity, it's not difficult to detect what your partner enjoys. Chances are, your partner is kissing you the way he or she wishes to be kissed.

ORIGIN OF THE KISS

♥

If you think about it, giving someone a kiss is a rather bizarre act. You are taking your mouth—a damp, germ-infested opening through which food (and who knows what else) passes—and touching another with it. Where did this kissing business originate, and why isn't it a rubbing of bellies or a fondling of elbows instead?

Who's responsible for the first kiss? How did they come up with such an idea? And how did they talk someone else into doing it with them?

Surprisingly, there is very little historical information on kissing to answer these questions. One famous adventurer claims that the kiss is "as old as creation, and yet as young and fresh as ever. It pre-existed, still exists, and always will exist." Despite the absence of factual information, there are several theories floating around that try to explain the origin of the kiss. Some hold water; others leak like a sieve.

One theory postulates that early humans discovered the cooling-down effect that salt consumption played on hot days. The skin of another person presented a very handy source of salt. Individuals taking advantage of this nearby resource licked the salt off one another, and this licking somehow evolved into current-day kissing. While this idea is creative, the notion that kissing resulted from an effort to cool down is hard to concede. Have *you* ever cooled off from kissing?

Kissing may have its roots in early religious rituals. Participants in ancient ceremonies used a form of the mouth kiss to exchange breath, which was believed to hold the soul and power of an individual. Thus the sharing of breath signified a conferring of power and a marriage of souls.

The kiss could also be a refinement of nose rubbing, which evolved from animal sniffing. Sociologists have noted that the literal translation of "kiss me" in certain tribes is "smell me." Further, Eskimos, Laplanders, and Polynesians are well known for the way they greet one another by pressing their noses together and inhaling. So it is possible that the kiss's lineage is rooted in the instinctive sniffing of animals. If you remember where you last observed animals instinctively sniffing each other, you will be glad that humans, like the kiss, have evolved.

There are some who feel the kiss could have developed from biting. Certain animals habitually bite one another during foreplay and the fulfillment of the sex act. Some anthropologists speculate that early humans (in their anthropoid stage of evolution) may have found it necessary to fasten on to their mates during coitus by using their teeth. Even today, many societies, ranging from the lowly to the most highly civilized, use the "love bite" when sexually aroused or during sexual activity. This hypothesis is the only one to hint at the kiss having a sexual origin.

A more recent theory poses kissing as an instinctive action with the purpose of transferring sebum between partners. (Sebum is a product of sebaceous skin glands, which are found throughout the skin surface but are more highly concentrated along the inside of the lips.) It follows that "love" may be nothing more than an addiction to another's sebum, and kissing is the vehicle through which you find your sebum of choice.

Now, before you dismiss this theory completely, there is actual research proving that eagles and some other birds bond through an exchange of sebum. During avian mating, the suitor chews a piece of food and then gives it to his mate. In experiments where the suitor's sebaceous glands were removed, the suitee merely pecked at the donor and then flew off.

But of all the theories on kissing, the most popular describes the kiss's origin as a maturation from our natural birth instinct to suck our mother's breast for nourishment. Kissing is possibly a leftover yearning for nourishment.

Manifestations resembling the kiss are also found among various lower animals. Snails, for instance, rub antennae. Birds use their beaks for a kind of caress. Dogs lick their masters as a form of affection. So human beings are not the only animal who enjoys this tactile activity.

The diverse theories on the kiss's origin are a product of many cultures that treat the kiss differently. For instance, in a large number of African cultures, there is a maternal kiss between mother and child, but no romantic kissing among adults. Before the introduction of Western customs, the Chinese felt the kiss was indecent both in public and behind closed doors. And the Japanese, though exposed to the kiss, chose to do without it until recently. Since different and diverging cultures choose not to participate in the romantic kiss, it is not likely the result of a more advanced form of culture or civilization.

Although there are several theories to explain the kiss's origin, the truth of the matter is there is very little documentation. Any attempt at resolution is merely speculation.

"There is no author of the first kiss. Kissing, like much other good things, is anonymous."

♥

KISSING QUOTES
FOR EVERY OCCASION

♥

This collection of quotes on the subject of kissing is guaranteed entertainment.

KISSING ACCORDING TO THE FAMOUS

"Political baby kissing must come to an end, unless the size and the age of the babies be materially increased."
    W. C. Fields

"Few men know how to kiss well; fortunately, I've always had time to teach them."
    Mae West

"I get no respect from my wife. She kisses the dog, but she won't drink out of my glass."
    Rodney Dangerfield

"What is a kiss? An inquiry on the second floor as to whether the first floor is free."
    Art Garfunkel

"The kiss originated when the first male reptile licked the first female reptile, implying in a subtle, complimentary way that she was as succulent as the small reptile he had for dinner the night before."

> *F. Scott Fitzgerald*

"Two people kissing always look like fish."

> *Andy Warhol*

"Everybody winds up kissing the wrong person good night."

> *Andy Warhol*

"A kiss on the wrist feels good, but a diamond bracelet lasts forever."

> *Adlai Stevenson, Address to Chicago Council on Foreign Relations, March 22, 1946*

"I wasn't kissing her, I was whispering in her mouth."

> *Chico Marx*

"I kissed my first woman and smoked my first cigarette on the same day. I have never had time for tobacco since."

> *Arturo Toscanini*

"You know Mr. [D. W.] Griffith told us we must never kiss actors —it isn't healthy."

> *Dorothy Gish*

KISSES FROM THE HEART

"You must remember this, a kiss is still a kiss,
A sigh is just a sigh;
The fundamental things apply,
As time goes by."
> Herman Hupfeld, Everybody's Welcome *(1931)*
> Also in the film Casablanca

"Give me a kisse and to that kisse a score;
Then to that twenty, add a hundred more:
And thousand to that hundred: so kisse on,
To make that thousand up a million;
Treble that million, and when that is done,
Let's kisse afresh, as when we first begun."
> Robert Herrick, "To Anthea: Oh, My Anthea"
> Hesperides *(1648)*

"Four sweet lips, two pure souls, and one undying affection—
these are love's pretty ingredients for a kiss."
> Christian Nestell Bovee

"A soft lip would tempt you to eternity of kissing!"
> Ben Jonson

"The splash of the waves against the pebbles of the beach is like
the sound of long kisses."
> Johannes Jorgensen

"The kiss you take is paid by that you give:
The joy is mutual, and I'm still in debt."
        Lord Lansdowne

"Hang up love's mistletoe over the earth,
And let us kiss under it all the year round."
        Anonymous

"A kiss is a rosy dot over the 'i' of loving."
        Cyrano de Bergerac

"Is not a kiss the very autograph of love?"
        Henry T. Finck

"Graze on my lips, and if those hills be dry,
Stray lower, where the pleasant fountains lie."
        William Shakespeare, Venus and Adonis

"That which you cannot give without taking and cannot take with-
out giving."
        Anonymous

"The sound of a kiss is not so loud as that of a cannon, but its
echo lasts a great deal longer."
        Oliver Wendell Holmes, The Professor at the
        Breakfast Table, *Chapter 11*

"Once he drew, with one long kiss,
My whole soul through my lips."
        Alfred, Lord Tennyson

"It is the passion that is in a kiss that gives to it its sweetness; it is the affection in a kiss that sanctifies it."
      Christian Nestell Bovee

"For love or lust, for good or ill,
Behold the kiss is potent still."
      John Richard Moreland, "The Kiss"

"I understand thy kisses, and thou mine,
And that's a feeling disputation."
      Shakespeare, Henry IV, Part I

"Kisses kept are wasted;
Love is to be tasted."
      Edmund Vance Cooke, "Kisses Kept are Wasted"

"A kiss that speaks volumes is seldom a first edition."
      Anonymous

Here's to the smoke that curls in the air
Here's to the dog at my feet;
Here's to the girls that have gone before,
Gad! but their kisses were sweet!
      Old drinking toast

KISSING WITTICISMS

"The honeymoon is over when the kiss that was a temptation becomes an obligation."
    Anonymous

"Lord, I wonder what fool it was that first invented kissing!"
    Jonathan Swift, "Polite Conversation"

"In fifty years kissing will be unheard of—but in fifty years, who cares?
    A prominent physician wishing to remain anonymous

"Lots of things have been started by kisses, especially young things."
    Anonymous

"Be plain in dress, and sober in your diet:
In short, my deary, kiss me, and be quiet."
    Lady Mary Wortley Montague

"Kissing is the most pleasant way of spreading germs yet devised."
    Anonymous

"To kiss or not to kiss is one of the most important questions of the twentieth century: a question which is normally answered no and acted yes."
    Dr. Albert Ellis

"Stealing a kiss may be petty larceny, but sometimes it's grand."
    Anonymous

"It's a good idea to kiss the children good night, if you don't mind waiting up for them."
    Anonymous

"A kiss is not enough for one, just enough for two, and too much for three."
    Anonymous

"Kissing is where two people get so close together they can't see anything wrong with each other."
    A psychologist wishing to remain anonymous

28

"There are certain tasks where you want personal interaction rather than dealing directly with a computer, like necking."
    Anonymous

"Traditional Hollywood style greeting for friend and foe alike."
    Eugene E. Brussell

LIP SERVICE

"If you kiss enough asses, you'll get kicked in the teeth."
Gerald Barzan

"Never a lip is curved with pain
That can't be kissed into smile again."
Bret Harte, "The Last Galleon"

"The greatest sin 'twixt heaven and hell
Is first to kiss and then to tell."
Anonymous

"The lips that have been innocent of passion's kiss frequently
ooze with gossip's poison."
Ella Wheeler Wilcox

"A kiss can be a comma, a question mark or an exclamation
point."
Mistinguette

"The hole in the face is called the mouth
For getting in and giving out,
For every kiss there is a bite,
The tongue hangs long, the lips lock tight."
Anonymous

"Do not make me kiss, and you will not make me sin."
H. G. Bohn, "Hand-Book of Proverbs"

"Stolen kisses are always sweetest."
Leigh Hunt

"A lisping lass is good to kiss."
Old proverb

"In love, there is always one who kisses and one who offers the cheek."
French proverb

"Formerly a kiss used to follow a nice evening, but nowadays a nice evening follows a kiss."
Anonymous

"Let us drink to the thought that wherever a man roves
He is sure to find something blissful and dear,
And that when he is far from the lips that he loves,
He can always make love to the lips that are near."
Tom Moore

"Before you kiss a handsome prince,
You have to kiss a lot of frogs."
20th-century proverb

"Wounds from a friend are better than kisses from an enemy!"
Proverbs 27:6

"A kiss without a mustache is like an egg without salt."
Old Spanish saying

"A man often kisses the hand he would rather cut off."
> *Spanish, Portuguese, Danish, Turkish, and Swahili proverb*

"Pretty red lips as soft as a rose
How many have kissed them God only knows."
> *Anonymous*

"To love platonically and to kiss is as absurd as a hunger-striker who would carry out his purpose by becoming a vegetarian."
> *Bauer*

"Benjy. The kiss. There are all sorts of kisses, lad, from the sticky confection to the kiss of death. Of them all, the kiss of an actress is the most unnerving. How can we tell if she means it or if she's just practicing?"
> *Ruth Gordon,* The Leading Lady, *Act II (1948)*

"We have kissed away kingdoms and provinces."
> *William Shakespeare,* Antony and Cleopatra

"The purest kiss in the world is this:
The kiss that a mother lays
On her boy's fresh lips
As he blithely trips
To meet the world and its ways."
> *Anonymous*

"Apple pie without some cheese
Is like a Kiss without a squeeze."
　　　Printed on the napkins of a diner

"Take heed that when upon her lips you seize,
You press them not too hard lest it displease."
　　　Ovid, "Art of Love"

"Kissing a smoker is like licking a dirty ashtray."
　　　Anonymous

HER SIDE—A FEMININE PERSPECTIVE

"To a woman the first kiss is the end of the beginning; to a man it is the beginning of the end."
　　　Helen Rowland, Reflections of a Bachelor Girl

"Marriage is the miracle that transforms a kiss from a pleasure into a duty."
　　　Helen Rowland

"A man snatches the first kiss, pleads for the second, demands the third, takes the fourth, accepts the fifth—and endures all the rest."
　　　Helen Rowland

"Every time some men plant a kiss they expect to reap a harvest."
  Anonymous

"The first kiss is stolen by the man; the last is begged by the woman."
  H. L. Mencken

"When a man tells you your kisses are intoxicating, watch out: he is probably mixing his drinks."
  Anonymous

"My child, if you finally decide to let a man kiss you, put your whole heart and soul into it. No man likes to kiss a rock."
  Lady Chesterfield

HIS SIDE—A MASCULINE PERSPECTIVE

"He who has stolen a kiss and knows not how to steal the rest deserves to forfeit his advantage."
  Ovid, "Art of Love"

"It's impossible to kiss a girl unexpectedly—only sooner than she thought you would."
  Anonymous

"I am in favor of preserving the French habit of kissing ladies' hands—after all, one must start somewhere."
      Sacha Guitry

"Don't wait to know her better to kiss her; kiss her, and you'll know her better."
      Anonymous

"If you are ever in doubt as to whether or not you should kiss a pretty girl, always give her the benefit of the doubt."
      Thomas Carlyle

"Any man who can drive safely while kissing a pretty girl is simply not giving the kiss the attention it deserves."
      Anonymous

"A man who kisses every girl he meets gets a lot of rebuffs—also a lot of kisses."
      Anonymous

"The trouble with girls who are highbrows is that they would rather be osculated than kissed."
      Anonymous

"Kissing a girl is like opening a jar of olives—hard to get the first one, but the rest come easy."
      Anonymous

"Kissing and bussing differ in this:
We buss our Wantons, but our Wives we kiss."
        Robert Herrick

"If your wife kisses you when you get home, is it affection or inspection?"
        Anonymous

"Some girls blush when they are kissed, and some swear; but the worst are those who laugh."
        Anonymous

"Alas! that women do not know
Kisses make men loath to go."
        Anonymous

"Kissing don't last; cookery do!"
        George Meredith

"A boy becomes a man when he decides it's more fun to steal a kiss than second base."
        Anonymous

"The difference between a man kissing his sister and a pretty girl is about fifty-five seconds."
        Anonymous

"Here's to the girl with eyes of brown,
If you ask for a kiss she will call you down;
Here's to the girl with eyes of blue,
If you ask for one—she will say, yes, take two."
                    Old drinking toast

"When women kiss, it always reminds me of prize-fighters shaking hands."
                    H. L. Mencken

SENTIMENTAL DEFINITIONS

"That which you cannot give without taking and cannot take without giving."
                    Anonymous

"It is a noun both common and proper,
Not very singular; and agrees with both you and me."
                    Anonymous

"A kiss is one of the most potent stimulants that a man or woman can indulge in."
                    Sheikh Nefzawi

"A kiss is the twenty-seventh letter of the alphabet . . . the love-labial which it takes two to speak plainly."
                    Oliver Wendell Holmes

"Soul meets soul on lover's lips."
                    Percy Bysshe Shelley

KISSING IN THE MOVIES

"Where do the noses go?"
>*Ingrid Bergman to Gary Cooper in* For Whom the
>Bell Tolls *(Paramount, 1943)*

"I love him because he doesn't know how to kiss—the jerk!"
>*Barbara Stanwyck about Gary Cooper in* Ball of Fire
>*(Fox, 1935)*

"It's even better when you help."
>*A critical Lauren Bacall speaking to a passive*
>*Humphrey Bogart in* To Have and Have Not *(Warner*
>*Brothers, 1944)*

*"Here's a soldier of the South who loves you, Scarlett, wants to
feel your arms around him, wants to carry the memory of your
kisses into battle with him. Never mind about loving me. You're
a woman sending a soldier to his death with a beautiful memory.
Scarlett, kiss me. Kiss me, once."*
>*Clark Gable leaving Vivien Leigh for war in* Gone
>With the Wind *(MGM, 1939)*

"Cross my heart, and kiss my elbow."
>*Audrey Hepburn in* Breakfast at Tiffany's
>*(Paramount, 1961)*

"There's something terribly uncomplimentary in apologizing for kissing a beautiful woman."

> Richard Arlen to Ida Lupino in Artists and Models
> (Paramount, 1937)

"Frankly, my child, I had a sudden, powerful and very ignoble desire to kiss you till your lips were somewhat bruised."

> David Niven bluntly confessing his desire to
> Maggie McNamara in The Moon Is Blue (United
> Artists, 1953)

"I will not have my face smeared with lipstick. If you want to kiss me, kiss me on the lips, which is what a merciful providence provided them for."

> Herbert Marshall speaking to Gene Tierney in
> The Razor's Edge (20th Century Fox, 1946)

"I don't know why I should act so experienced. It was only my second kiss this year."

> Diane Varsi making a confession to Russ Tamblyn
> in Peyton Place (20th Century Fox, 1957)

"From now on, I've got to know the name of every man that kisses me."

> Ida Lupino in Artists and Models (Paramount, 1937)

"Kissing your hand may make you feel very very good, but a diamond and sapphire bracelet lasts forever."

> Marilyn Monroe in Gentlemen Prefer Blondes (20th
> Century Fox, 1953)

Curtis: "Where did you learn to kiss like that?"
Monroe: "I used to sell kisses for the milk fund."
Curtis: "Tomorrow, remind me to send a check for $100,000 to
*   the milk fund."*
        Tony Curtis responding to a kiss from Marilyn
        Monroe in Some Like It Hot *(United Artists, 1959)*

"I have a message for your wife. Don't wipe it off. If she thinks
that's cranberry sauce, tell her she's got cherry pits in her head."
        Marilyn Monroe sending Tom Ewell back to his wife
        with a kiss in The Seven Year Itch *(20th Century Fox,*
        1955)

"Just because I kiss you—does that make me your girl?"
        Doris Day in The Pajama Game *(Warner Brothers,*
        1957)

39

"Come on, give your mommy a big sloppy kiss."
        Elizabeth Taylor to Richard Burton in Who's Afraid
        of Virginia Woolf? *(Warner Brothers, 1966)*

"I'd love to kiss you, but I just washed my hair."
        Bette Davis to Richard Barthelmess in Cabin in the
        Cotton *(Warner Brothers, 1932)*

"I'd just as soon kiss a Wookie."
        Carrie Fisher to Harrison Ford in The Empire
        Strikes Back *(Fox, 1980)*

"That was restful. Again."
> A Russian Greta Garbo allowing Melvyn Douglas
> to teach her the Western custom of kissing in
> Ninotchka *(MGM, 1939)*

"When a woman kisses me, Louise, she has to take pot luck."
> Van Heflin to Joan Crawford in Possessed *(Warner
> Brothers, 1947)*

*"When a clumsy cloud from here meets a fluffy little cloud from
there, he billows towards her. She scurries away, and he scuds
right up to her. She cries a little, and there you have your shower.
He comforts her. They spark. That's the lightning. They kiss.
Thunder!"*

> Fred Astaire warming up Ginger Rogers in Top Hat
> *(RKO Radio, 1935)*

"Don't tell me it's subversive to kiss a Republican."
> John Lund romancing an Iowa Congresswoman
> *(Jean Arthur)* in A Foreign Affair *(Paramount, 1948)*

"Now I have kissed you through two centuries."
> Laurence Olivier romancing Vivien Leigh into the
> nineteenth century in That Hamilton Woman *(United
> Artists, 1941)*

KISSING DITTIES

Kiss and hug
Kiss and hug,
Smack your sweetie
On the mug.

Kiss beneath the garden gate,
Kiss beneath a rose,
But the proper place to kiss a boy
Is right beneath the nose.

Pucker your lips
And close your eyes,
You're going to get
A big surprise!

Johnny and Susie
Sitting in a tree
K-I-S-S-I-N-G
First comes love,
Then comes marriage,
Then comes junior
In a baby carriage.

Snuggle snuggle
Smooch and smack,
Kissing's fine
And that's a fact.

41

♥

KISSING FACTS & TRIVIA

♥

KISSING RECORDS

Long-Term Kissing World Record According to the *Guinness Book of World Records*, the holders of this title are Bobbie Sherlock and Ray Blazina. The kiss lasted 130 hours and 2 minutes, and was performed at the 1978 "Smoochathon" held in Pittsburgh for the benefit of cystic fibrosis. (GBWR)

Longest Kiss Ever Lasted 17 days, 10.5 hours. It was performed in Chicago on September 24, 1984, by Eddie Levin, and Delphine Crha, 26. They celebrated the event with, what else, a kiss. (GBWR).

Longest Kiss Underwater Was performed for Fuji TV in Tokyo, Japan, on April 2, 1980. Toshiaki Shirai and Yukiko Nagata kissed underwater for 2 minutes, 18 seconds. (GBWR)

Most Women Kissed in Succession On May 30, 1988, James Whale, at the Yorkshire TV Telethon garden party in Leeds, England, kissed 4,525 women in 8 hours. That was one kiss every 6.36 seconds. (GBWR)

Kiss of Life   From August 27 to September 9, 1984, five members of the St. John Ambulance team from Australia maintained mouth-to-mouth resuscitation, or the "kiss of life," for 315 hours. A total of 232,150 inflations were counted by the "patient," who was a dummy. (GBWR)

MOVIE KISSES

First Movie Kiss   Was performed in 1896 by May Irwin and John C. Rice for a thirty-second nickelodeon production by Thomas Edison entitled "The Kiss."

The Most Kisses in Any One Movie   John Barrymore in Warner Brothers' 1926 production of *Don Juan*. A total of 191 kisses were recorded with two-thirds going to the two co-stars, Mary Astor and Estelle Taylor.

Longest Kiss in Cinematic History   Regis Toomey and Jane Wyman performed a 185-second kiss in the 1940 release of *You're in the Army Now*. This kiss, which lasted a little over three minutes, represented 4 percent of the movie's length.

Big Screen Kissing   The Screen Actors Guild in October of 1985 issued a policy statement that open-mouthed kissing could be "possibly hazardous work." This was in reaction to Rock Hudson kissing Linda Evans in the television show "Dynasty," shortly before he died of AIDS. Actors now must be told if their roles require open-mouthed kissing before being hired.

CELEBRITIES ON KISSING

Kisses of Mae West   In an interview with Associated Press in 1968, Mae West confessed to never actually kissing a man during any of her performances on stage, and rarely doing so in films. She stated: "I always felt that the look before the kiss was more important than the kiss itself. I figured it was better to fade out before the kiss and let the audience use its imagination."

Maurice Chevalier   Was once asked why the French kiss friends of either sex on the cheek. He answered, "It is simply that we like to renew acquaintances, we Frenchmen. We may kiss a man we haven't seen for five years—or a girl we haven't seen for five minutes."

44

Author James Joyce   After writing *Ulysses*, James Joyce was asked by a young man if he could kiss the hand that wrote such a great work. Joyce responded "No," then added "it did lots of other things too."

Bob Hope   When asked by a reporter to describe what it was like working in television opposite Lucille Ball, who at the time was president of Desilu, Hope responded, "I never thought I'd be kissing the president of a company—on the lips."

More Bob Hope   A woman who once kissed Bob Hope asked him, "How did you ever learn to kiss like that?" "It comes natural, I guess," he replied. "I blow up all my own motorcycle tires."

STUDIES ON KISSING

Number of Men Kissed Before Marriage According to Dr. Joyce Brothers, the average American female has kissed seventy-nine men before she is married.

Call Girls and Kissing Sex therapist Martha Stein studied sixty-four call girls and their clients to understand the association between deep kissing and emotional closeness of the middle class. While hidden in the bedroom, Stein observed 1,230 sexual encounters. Only 36 percent of the encounters included tongue kissing.

Kinsey Report According to Kinsey, the French kiss is utilized the least in American culture by adult males whose education level does not exceed the eighth grade.

Germs and Kissing Students from Baltimore City College in the late 1950s conducted an experiment in which they analyzed glass slides that they had kissed to determine what germs might be passed by kissing. They discovered that as many as 278 colonies of bacteria were passed during a kiss. Fortunately, 95 percent of the transmitted colonies were found to be completely harmless.

Kiss Your Wife! Statistics have shown that men who kiss their wives good-bye in the morning live five years longer than those who don't.

AIDS and Kissing Though the AIDS virus can be found in saliva, there have been no recorded cases where kissing has resulted in transmission of the virus.

The "Kissing Disease" The nickname given to mononucleosis, a disease with symptoms of fatigue, fever, sore throat, and enlarged lymph glands, and lasting usually two to six weeks. Because its precise method of transmission is unknown, speculation by many has established that the disease is transmitted by oral contact when there is salivary interchange, as in kissing.

LITTLE-KNOWN KISSING FACTS

Kisses of the Buddhist It was reported that a devout Buddhist on his final six-mile pilgrimage to Lhasa will kiss the ground over 30,000 times. (*"The Origin of the Kiss"* by Surgeon C. M. Beadnell)

46 *Kissing Fish* Called "kissing gourami," these are tropical fish with either pink or green-white color. They actually kiss their own kind on the mouth, and their kissing has been reported to last up to twenty-five minutes.

No-Kissing Zone Wives who drove their husbands to the train station in Deerfield, Illinois, were stopping traffic to kiss their husbands good-bye. To solve this traffic problem the city created two zones fifty feet apart. They labeled the zones "Kissing" and "No Kissing."

Anti-Kissing League In 1909 a group of men from Kansas formed the Anti-Kissing League. These men viewed kissing as unhealthy and unnecessary, and pledged to never again kiss their wives. The league shortly after disbanded.

The Blue Laws The famous Connecticut blue laws prohibited kissing—even by married couples—on Sundays and fast days.

Kissing in Washington, D.C. This reached an all-time high during the Carter years.

Kiss of Peace St. Paul is credited with creating the kiss of peace. He instructed his followers to "salute one another with a holy kiss," during Christian services, baptism, confession, ordination, and communion.

Porcupine Kiss North American porcupines have their own version of a courtship kiss. The male and female nuzzle each other's noses, which are one of the few places free of quills.

47

Mr. Kiss A Hungarian-American pharmacist, Max Kiss, is credited with combining chocolate with a laxative. He called it "Excellent Laxative," which was later shortened to Ex-Lax.

Opera dilemma Sir Rudolf Bing, former opera administrator at the New York's Metropolitan Opera, was faced with a flu epidemic spreading through the cast. His solution was to post a sign that read "Confine your kissing to the irresistible." *(The Little Brown Book of Anecdotes)*

Kissing Tellers A bank in Seattle posted a sign that read: "Don't kiss our girls—they're All Tellers!"

Airport Kisses The New Orleans airport was having a problem with passengers delaying flights. It therefore posted the sign: "Start kissing good-bye early, so the plane can leave on time."

KISSING CUSTOMS

Mistletoe The origin of the tradition of kissing under the mistletoe during the Christmas season cannot be clearly traced. The closest explanation comes from a Scandinavian myth. Baldur, god of light and spring, dreamed that his life was in danger. His mother, Frigga, goddess of love, gained promises from Earth, Air, Fire and Water that they would not hurt her son. However, she forgot about mistletoe, the parasitic plant which does not grow from any of the four elements. Loki, god of fire, was jealous of Baldur, so he had him slain with a dart of mistletoe. In her grief, Frigga decreed that mistletoe would never again be used as a weapon, and promised to place a kiss on anyone who passed under it.

XXX Those "X's" at the bottom of letters to symbolize kisses originated in the Middle Ages. The illiterate would draw an "X" on the signature line of a contract when they couldn't sign their name and then kiss the contract to show sincerity. Eventually the "X" itself came to signify a kiss.

Blowing a Kiss The practice of blowing kisses to departing friends started in 3,000 B.C., during the Sargonic dynasty, in Mesopotamia when pagan worshipers used this gesture to throw kisses to their pagan gods.

The Wedding Kiss　The initial purpose behind the nuptial kiss was to symbolize the spiritual union between bride and groom. The kiss was the vehicle for exchanging the "breath of life." During medieval times, the wedding kiss held legal significance. Should one of the two die before the kiss, all wedding gifts had to be returned. However, once the two exchanged the *osculum interveniens*, the presents stayed.

KISSING TERMINOLOGY

Philematology　The study of kissing.

Osculation　The act of kissing.

Maraichinage　Another word for deep kissing or French kissing. Comes from a group of people called the Maraichins who lived in Marais, a region in western France that borders on the Bay of Biscay. The deep kiss was very popular there.

Lipograph　Invented by David Bowie in 1979, when he sent a lipstick imprint of his kiss on an autographed card to a cosmetic firm publicist as a thank-you gesture. The publicist, inspired by the lipograph, convinced eighty more celebrities to create lipographs, which were auctioned off to benefit the Save the Children Foundation. The charitable event collected $16,000. The most expensive lipographs included Mick Jagger's for $1,600, and Marlene Dietrich's for $1,200.

Osculum　Latin for a kiss on the face or cheek between friends.

Basium　Latin for a kiss on the lips as a sign of affection.

Suavium or Savium   A Latin word meaning a kiss between the lips. Refers to a kiss between lovers.

KISSING ACRONYMS AND ABBREVIATIONS

C.Y.K.   consider yourself kissed
KISS   keep it simple, stupid; or keep it simple and stupid
SWAK   sealed with a kiss
Q.B.S.P.   *que besa sus pies* (Spanish for "Who kisses your feet")
Q.B.S.M.   *que besa su mano* (Spanish for "Who kisses your hand")

IDIOMATIC PHRASES

Hollywood Kiss   To dismiss or get rid of someone. "Kiss off." Used primarily on the East Coast, especially in New York City.

Kiss a Cow   To verify the truth.

Kiss and Make Up   To forgive and be friends again. It is believed to have originated in societies where a kiss of reconciliation precedes the handshake. Also used literally.

Kiss and Tell   Telling others about your romantic moments which should be kept secret.

Kiss Black Betty   Drinking liquor to excess.

Kiss (Something or Someone) Good-bye   To anticipate or experience the loss of something.

Kiss Me, Sergeant World War I British army expression, a common jesting uttered after an officer has been somewhat serious about his rank. Was also said to the orderly sergeant in army camps after he commanded "lights out!"

Kiss My Ass American and Canadian (kiss my arse). A catchall phrase of profound contempt or an intensified negative. Dating back to 1860.

Kiss My Foot Rubbish. Mostly an Australian and Canadian expression of the nineteenth and twentieth century.

Kiss My Grits An intensified negative. Same meaning as "drop dead," or "go jump in the lake."

Kiss My Tail A violently contemptuous retort of eighteenth- to twentieth-century usage. Obsolete by 1960.

Kiss My Tuna An all-purpose exclamation of rejection. Used primarily by "Valley Girls."

Kiss of Death Made famous by Alfred E. Smith in a speech describing William Randolph Hearst's support of Ogden Mills (1926). Also from Judas Iscariot's kissing of Christ in the great betrayal scene, thenceforth to any other callous betrayal. Applied to a fatal or extremely dangerous contact.

Kiss Off To dismiss, or get rid of something or someone, often rudely and curtly.

Kiss One's Aircraft Good-bye   To bail out. From the RAF (Royal Air Force) aircrew of World War II.

Kiss Out   To be denied or cheated out of one's share of the profits.

Kiss the Baby (Babe)   To take a drink.

Kiss the Book   To take the oath.

Kiss the Bottle   To drink liquor.

Kiss the Canvas   Also "kiss the resin." A boxing term meaning to be knocked out.

52   *Kiss the Claws*   To salute.

Kiss the Counter   To be confined to prison.

Kiss the Cross   To be knocked out, as in boxing.

Kiss the Dog   To pick a pocket while facing the victim.

Kiss the Dust   To die, to be defeated, or to be overthrown.

Kiss the Ground   To be humiliated, or to be thrown off a horse.

Kiss the Gunner's Daughter   To be tied to the ship's cannon and caned.

Kiss the Hare's Foot To be too late for meals. Probably meant that one coming to partake of the hare had no better chance but to kiss the hare's foot than to get something to eat.

Kiss the Maid To lose one's head in a guillotine; mid-eighteenth-century expression.

Kiss the Porcelain God To vomit.

Kiss the Shilling To be cheap (penny kisser).

Kisser Wiper A strike to the face.

New York Kiss To dismiss or get rid of someone. Used on the West Coast; especially in Los Angeles.

Play Kissie To be falsely friendly and flattering to another.

KISSING GEOGRAPHY

FOREHEAD Respect
CHEEK Friendship and affection
HAND Homage
FOOT Reverence and humility
MOUTH Love

KISSING SUPERSTITIONS

Kiss over a gate, you'll have bad luck.

If your nose itches, you'll be kissed by a fool.

Kissing a deck of cards before playing insures winning.

A kiss from a chimney sweep will bring good luck.

Sneeze on Tuesday, you'll kiss a stranger.

Crossing your heart and kissing the ground three times prevents being struck by lightning.

Kiss your elbow and you'll change your sex.

If a sitting woman and a standing man kiss each other, they'll quarrel.

If a bride doesn't cry when the groom first kisses her at the ceremony, their marriage will be unhappy.

Kissing in a gondola under the Bridge of Sighs in Venice at sunset while the bells of the Campanile toll will bestow eternal love on the couple.

KISSING DRINKS

A Widow's Kiss   (Brandy drink)

1 oz. 5 star Brandy
½ oz. Chartreuse (yellow)

½ oz. Benedictine
1 dash bitters

Shake with ice and strain into cocktail glass.

Soul Kiss Cocktail   (Vermouth)

1½ tsp. orange juice
1½ tsp. Dubonnet

¾ oz. dry vermouth
¾ oz. Bourbon

Shake with ice and strain into cocktail glass.

Kiss-in-the-Dark   (Vermouth)

¾ oz. gin
¾ oz. cherry-flavored brandy

¾ oz. dry vermouth

Stir with ice and strain into cocktail glass.

Kiss the Boys Good-bye   (Brandy)

¾ oz. gin
¾ oz. 5 Star Brandy

½ egg white
juice of 1 lemon

Shake with ice and strain into cocktail glass.

Angel's Kiss   (Pousse-café)

¼ oz. Gremede Cacao (white)
¼ oz. gin

¼ oz. 5 Star Brandy
¼ oz. light cream

Pour ingredients carefully into pousse-café glass, in the order given, so they don't mix. (Pousse-cafés are sweet, striped drinks made by pouring a series of liqueurs in succession so that one floats on top of another.)

A Summer's Kiss   (Mixed drink)

1 oz. Amaretto

3 oz. cranberry juice

Pour over ice into glass.

Kissing Hierarchy In the Middle Ages, rank determined where you would kiss someone in greeting. The lower you were on the status pole, the farther from the face you moved. You'd kiss peers on the mouth, those a notch above you on the hand, those higher still on the knee, and those to whom you were merely dust (primarily religious figures) you kissed on the foot or the ground at their feet. This is where the phrase "I kiss the ground you walk on" originates.

Kiss of Trust The earliest kiss of greeting was a sign of great trust. You were allowing someone close enough to show you did not fear the person would bite your ear or stab you in the back.

Kissing Alternatives London's Great Plague of 1665 (which lasted almost a year and killed 68,596) put a damper on the popular act of social kissing. The fear of catching something from a neighbor made tipping hats, bowing, curtsying, and waving hands the new popular greeting gestures.

P.D.A. (Public Display of Affection) Public kissing was highly discouraged in American etiquette books until well into this century. Our current casual attitude toward public kissing is a result of an increased exposure to other cultures who openly kiss in public.

The Upper Crust Historically, social kissing has been most common among the elite.

An Expression of Love Historians are quite certain that expressing love with a kiss is a rather recent phenomenon. Greek poetry scarcely mentions it, and there is no word for kissing in any of the Celtic languages.

Christian Kiss The kiss as a Christian ritual was introduced during the Middle Ages. As a result, women began to freely kiss their male friends.

Medieval Adultery A Medieval French law stated that a married woman was guilty of adultery if she kissed or allowed herself to be kissed by a man other than her husband.

The Kissing King King Louis XII of France was famous for kissing every woman in Normandy, using the sham of granting his Royal Benediction.

Kiss and Be Hitched During the Middle Ages Italians took a kiss very seriously. If a man kissed a girl in public, he could become obliged to marry her.

Kissing Archeology The earliest known representation of a deep kiss dates back to around 200 B.C. It was found on erotic Mochica pottery in Peru.

Kissing Romans In ancient Rome, the kiss was used to greet not only friends and family but also shopkeepers, salespeople, and the general population.

Kissing and the Law A Roman law, during the imperial period, gave a man legal rights to a woman (including sanctions if the marriage plans were canceled) as soon as he gave her a betrothal kiss.

A Kissless Lover Kissing was almost unknown in ancient Egypt. Cleopatra, the great lover, is believed not to have kissed any of her numerous conquests.

A Loving Kiss Credit for the development of the romantic kiss is given to India shortly after the time of the Aryan penetration.

LIP FACTS

What Are Lips? Lips are a transition skin layer between the outer hair-bearing tissue and the inner mucous membrane. They have a high concentration of sensitive nerve endings, which explains why it is so enjoyable to have them lightly touched.

The Perfect Lips Good news. There is no such thing. The "in" lip shape changes with each generation.

Lipstick Lipstick is a simple formulation of oil, pigment, and wax. The oil permits the spreading and sticking, the pigment creates the color, and the wax supplies the rigidity necessary for molding into a stick. The difference between lipstick and lip gloss is the presence of more wax in the stick and more oil in the gloss.

Chapped Lips Fix Touch lips with a warm wash cloth until they feel soft. Rub a generous layer of petroleum jelly on the lips and allow to set for three minutes. Gently rub lips with a warm wash cloth to sluff away any loose or dry skin. Apply a creamy lipstick or lip protection cream. Blot and apply a second coat.

❤ BASIC KISSONYMS ❤

BUSS	HONEY COOLER	PECK
CANOODLE	KISSAROO	PLANT A BURNER
DO A FADE OUT	KISSELTOE (DONE UNDER	PORCH PECK
FIRST BASE	THE MISTLETOE)	RUB SMACKERS
GAB GOOBER	LIP LOCK	SMACK
GATHER LIP ROUGE	LIP SALUTE	SMASH MOUTH
GIVE LIP	LOVE PECK	TACTION
GOOBER	MAKE A PASS	
HANG A GOOBER	OSCULATE	

kissing
basics

♥

A FIRST KISS

♥

The lights dim, and a sultry melody begins. A tall, handsome man grasps a shapely, dew-eyed woman in his arms. A seemingly endless pause of longing glances ensues, until slowly their eyes close and their mouths move toward one another. At last, their lips touch in a crash of cymbals and bursting fireworks. Their first kiss was perfect.

A first kiss like this only happens in the movies or in the imagination of some woebegone romantic. The truth about the first romantic kiss is that more often than not it's an awkward, blundering affair: clumsy touching, incorrect nose placement, and designer earring jabs.

A first kiss *can* be an incredibly exhilarating experience, when performed right. Unfortunately, most of us failed to inherit the "James Bond genius" for knowing where, when, and how to kiss someone for the first time so that the person is left spellbound. What needs to be done to make a first kiss a triumph instead of a tragedy?

Assuming you've chosen the right person, have you also chosen the right place and the right time? If your partner feels the place is inappropriate, it can spell immediate disaster. Most people, for example, don't like kissing or being kissed in public. This is commonly referred to as a "P.D.A." (public display of affection). A P.D.A. also includes kissing when there is an audience: friends, family, or co-workers. It's also hard to concentrate on kissing in an atmosphere where the more immediate concern is safety, such as when driving a moving car, or while preparing to disengage from a ski lift. And try to avoid kissing in a place of questionable privacy like an elevator, where the door could open at any minute. Granted, these unpredictable situations can generate excitement, but the first kiss is trying enough without having to worry about surprises.

A successful location for a first kiss is anywhere you are able to concentrate wholly on your partner. To that end, it should be private and comfortable, perhaps with romantic lighting or a pretty view. You should also give some thought to temperature. Obviously, if it's too hot, more concern is given to perspiration stains and body odor than to romance. In a cooler environment, however, you can make a convincing argument for getting close to your partner, either in an effort to get warm or to demonstrate caring for the other person's obvious discomfort. So consider turning down the thermostat. Then, at the first sign of goose bumps, come to your partner's aid.

As for timing, there are obvious moments when it's best to observe restraint. It's no fun to kiss when you're late for an appointment with a $100-an-hour plumber or working under a close deadline at the office. If your potential partner is on the phone reciting a sequence of numbers that might win a free trip to the Virgin Islands, don't interrupt. What if, when President Bush was saying "Read my lips," Barbara Bush was trying to kiss them? The right time is when there is time to do it right.

So, you're now at the point of having decided that it's the right person, the perfect place, and the proper time. Both of you are ready for the "big kiss." How do you make sure you don't blow it?

The biggest blunder is rushing into an intensely passionate first kiss with the belief that it will excite or overwhelm your partner. Kissing is not like an Olympic event, when speed wins the medal. So avoid zooming in with your mouth wide open, tongue at the ready, and with a crazed look in your eyes.

It is safer to approach a first kiss slowly, tentatively, with an exploratory touch of the lips permitting both partners the opportunity to decide whether to proceed with the activity. If one feels reluctant, the situation is recoverable with minimum embarrassment to either party. The slow and easy approach also helps you get to know one another. Experimenting with different kisses and touches, both partners will discover each other's preferences. Reducing a kiss's intensity and speed also demonstrates respect for the other person. You establish a trust which leads to a more relaxed and comfortable atmosphere. And performing at a slower pace lets the special moment last even longer.

Another stumbling block with a first kiss is over-aggressiveness. Inflicting a deep kiss too soon, impersonating an octopus, or removing clothing with your teeth are all overly aggressive actions. Any time you display dominance over the situation and your aim is self-gratification rather than pleasing your partner, this is over-aggressive behavior.

A woman kissing a man for the first time leaves lipstick traces all over his face. She doesn't care that he looks like Bozo the Clown. She is more interested in covering surface area.

A man, so self-consumed by his pleasure, doesn't comprehend that he is obstructing the only two openings through which his partner exchanges oxygen. She is breathless—but it's not from euphoria.

Remember, there are two of you kissing, and both should be participating and enjoying. The synergism of two far outweighs a solo act.

THE FIRST-KISS PROCESS

With the basic do's and don'ts of a first kiss covered, let's move on to successfully executing the kiss. This series of steps was designed so that you will err on the conservative side, if at all. The goal is to deliver an impressive first kiss while minimizing the awkward moments. Please note, however, that there is no singular *right* way to kiss someone for the first time.

Let's walk through the steps, expanding on each's relevance in the first-kiss process. Use the flowchart on page 68–69.

Decision to Kiss Here you are, in the company of someone you are desperate to kiss. Well, unless your partner is a mind reader, nothing is going to happen if you don't take some initiative. Make the decision.

Physical Contact Take a reading on your partner's interest in the idea. You can do this with a gentle touch: try either holding the person's hand, walking arm-in-arm, or sitting close. If you sense disapproval, smile, drop whatever you may be holding, and proceed with light conversation. (You have not yet put yourself in an embarrassing position, and you now have time to reevaluate the situation and perhaps try again later.)

Establish a Position If he or she is responding positively to your physical contact, the next step is positioning yourself so that you'll feel comfortable kissing your partner. In most situations, the optimal position is face-to-face with shoulders squared and body heights equal, either standing or sitting. It is preferable not to hold on to your partner, however; if you choose a hold, make sure it is nonthreatening. Your partner should never feel confined or restrained.

Eye Contact The eyes are capable of giving great insight into how your partner is feeling. Try to establish eye contact. If your eyes are not met, or eye contact is broken quickly, this is a signal to retreat. If the eye contact is sustained, move on to the next step.

Move in Closer   You are comfortably positioned, and you have strong eye contact. Now is the time to move in for the kiss. This is the final checkpoint prior to kissing. As you move in, pause slightly before touching the lips to see if your partner is also moving forward. You should be pausing around the time your partner's nose falls out of focus and you're forced to tilt your head to avoid a nose collision. The other party ought to make an ever-so-slight advance to let you know they are in agreement. If this doesn't happen, you may continue to the next step, or take the conservative approach—draw back and reexamine your partner's eyes.

Kiss   With a positive response from your partner, it is now time to approach for a romantic mouth-to-mouth kiss. Slowly and thoughtfully ease forward until the lips gently touch. Don't complicate the situation by bringing your tongue into play.

67

Stop   As the initiator of the kiss you should be the one to end it. It is considered bad form if your partner has to break away. Do not be abrupt, and in no way signal the end to further kissing. Simply pull back and observe your partner's eyes. If you move forward to continue with the kissing and your partner does not, this is a sign that perhaps he or she doesn't feel any chemistry. In this situation, it is advised that you stop kissing.

These steps are merely guidelines to performing a first kiss. Establishing physical contact could mean hugging, sharing ice cream, reading a menu together, or holding hands. You can get a quick "willingness" reading by asking your partner to dance with you to a slow song. How about inviting the person to your place to help cook a meal? (If the kitchen is small enough, you can't help but make physical contact.) Adapt these guidelines to suit your own personality and style.

FLOW OF A FIRST KISS

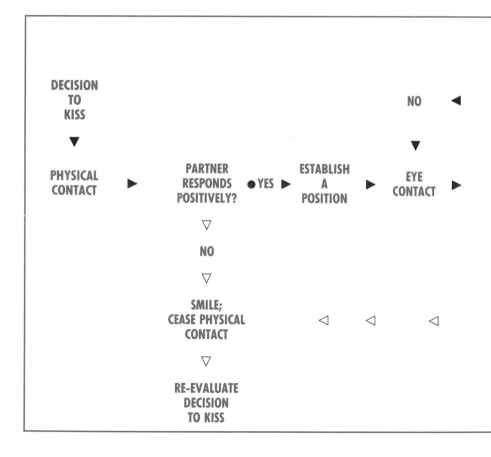

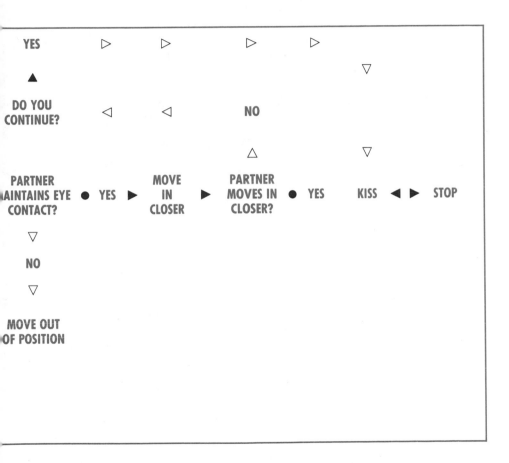

A FIRST DEEP KISS

Now that you've successfully performed a first kiss, it's time for pay dirt: the notorious French kiss, or deep kiss.

Beginning a deep kiss is much like knocking on someone's front door. The way you knock can determine whether you are invited inside. With your partner relaxed and responding affirmatively to your kisses, try parting your lips. Unless he or she pulls back, you might try gently touching the person's lips with your tongue. If you meet resistance, reel in your tongue, bring your lips back together, and resume kissing as you were earlier.

Don't interpret resistance as an unequivocal no. It's just a decision to hold off for now. Don't aggravate the situation by asking for an explanation; it leaves you wide open for some unflattering truth, like "I couldn't continue because your breath is like three-day-old cat food." Holding off will also increase your chances of having a second chance some other time.

On the flip side, if your partner responds to your "knocking" by parting lips, consider this gesture an invitation for your tongue to enter the mouth, and go on in, gradually. It is poor technique to thrust your tongue headlong into the mouth at a speed that could break the sound barrier or dental work. Proceed slowly and tentatively. The tongue contains very sensitive nerve endings; a light touch can cause quite a sensation.

The initiator now moves the tongue forward only as far as is necessary to meet the recipient's tongue. Once the tongues meet, each should massage the other in a tender caress. (See page 72, "Anatomy of a Kiss.") When the two of you begin to feel comfortable kissing this way, you can return to simple kissing, or advance to more involved "hot tonguing."

Proper deep kissing has three basic rules:

Account for Your Own Expectorate (Spit).

When you're nervous or excited you produce excess saliva. To avoid sending backwash into your partner's mouth, or drooling excessively, maintain a continuous light suction while deep kissing, and periodically break away to pause, swallow, and catch your breath.

Avoid Gagging Your Partner.

Your tongue should remain in your partner's mouth and not wander down the throat.

Don't "Over-French."

Returning to simple kissing does not mean losing ground. Participating in a lengthy deep kiss can be as tedious as listening to a record skip. And your lips start to feel like raisins. The wise kisser orchestrates his or her kissing session with an artful combination of deep and simple kisses to create crescendos and diminuendos. Variation keeps your partner attentive.

Just remember that after the first kiss, the two of you enter into a whole new relationship, with a new set of rules. Future kisses will never be quite like the first, so make every effort to treat this event as a special, unpredictable moment and strive to create a fabulous memory.

"The dearest remembrance will still be the best,
Our sweetest memorial the first kiss of love."
    Lord Byron

❤

ANATOMY OF A KISS

❤

It's always disappointing to find a new partner whose kissing could qualify as an orthodontic alternative to your overbite, or someone who kisses a path to your ear only to blow into it as if taking a breathalizer test. If your partner is a poor kisser, or you know of someone who is, take heart and read on.

LIPS

As major players in the sport of kissing, your lips ensure that the kiss comes across soft and moist. Contrary to popular thought, lips should *not* be puckered during a romantic kiss or the lips muscles will contract, forming a hard wrinkled nodule that feels like a doorknob.

With the lips relaxed, part them just enough so that they do not touch. (Some kissers overcorrect this point and kiss with their lips opened too far, producing the sensation of being gummed by a carp.) The lips should flare slightly outward to expose a hint of the inner lips. This inner lip is what gives a kiss its warm and moist quality. Think about how you hold your lips when drinking from a water fountain.

It is very important that your lips touch the lips of your partner *softly*. Smashing your partners' lips against their teeth not only reduces lip sensitivity; it is *very* painful, and is the most common complaint women have about men's kissing.

A deep kiss requires you to spread the lips further apart, allowing the tongue to pass in and out of the mouth freely. Frequently the lips will roll back and expose the hazardous teeth, which may catch or pinch lips, or bite into gums, causing your partner undue pain. While it may be difficult to concentrate on lips, tongue, and teeth simultaneously, you are the best off ensuring that each is in its proper place.

Once you have the basic lip position mastered, don't get stuck in a puckering rut. Beginning with the basic position, you can work together to come up with some unique hybrids such as kissing with your lower lips pouting, or with both pairs of lips so overcontracted that the two of you look like blow fish. Part of the fun of kissing is coming up with new variations or creating kisses that are for the two of you.

MOUTH

The mouth cavity houses the tongue, gums, and teeth, and the lips form its external boundaries. It goes without saying that this area needs to be clean and odor-free and you should remove any extraneous matter such as gum, chewing tobacco, sewing pins, toothpicks, and anything else foreign. Odor-free means void of onions, peanuts, smoke, beer, and anything else you wouldn't want to be tasting second-hand. (See page 89, "Breathless Kissing," for a more detailed discussion.)

You'll also need to think about spit control. Those who've experienced it know there's nothing worse than taking a face bath. Excessive saliva results from nervousness, excitement, or holding your breath, and can be avoided if you maintain a light suction while kissing. The suction you generate to drink from a straw, which is the same suction you use in kissing, solves two problems: it prevents your saliva from escaping into your partner's mouth (or worse, down his or her face), and it forces you to breathe. You should also try to pause occasionally between kisses, so you'll have time to swallow and catch your breath.

TONGUE

It is bad form to sit mouth open, tongue extended as if in a dentist chair, expecting your partner to do all the tongue work. On the other hand, too much tongue activity could leave your partner's tongue feeling as if it were caught in a food processor. A deep kiss is like two tongues slow dancing. The manner should be tender and endearing, and the movements should be slow, smooth, rhythmic, and varied, with neither party forcing control. Try licking peanut butter off the end of your finger and notice the way your tongue maneuvers to remove it. This, and licking a popsicle are the closest comparisons to proper tongue motion in a deep kiss.

Concentrate on touching the more sensitive membrane on the walls of the mouth rather than focusing on the teeth. Keep your tongue inside either mouth, and do not venture underneath your partner's tongue because more sensitive nerve endings are found on top of the tongue.

TASTE

The mouth is used to sense taste, yet rarely do we consider incorporating this function in kissing, which can take on a whole new twist if you can find ways to titillate your tongue's sensory preceptors. For instance, have you ever kissed someone after they've been sucking on an ice cube or drinking hot chocolate? Try experimenting with different flavors of liqueurs, or coffee. Cover your teeth with honey, chocolate syrup, peanut butter, even toothpaste—something you know your partner likes—and have him or her kiss you until it's gone. It's also a great way to experiment with new tongue techniques. Keep in mind that the consistency of the food you pick is very important: Oatmeal, scrambled eggs, or half-chewed popcorn have no visual appeal.

During your next kissing encounter, experiment with taste and temperature.

EYES

Most people kiss with their eyes closed. This is partly instinctive and partly because it is almost impossible to keep your partner in focus without going cross-eyed. Kissing closed-eyed also eliminates visual distractions so you're able to concentrate on the kiss itself.

You should close your eyes right after the head tilts and just before the lips touch to avoid a nose crash.

Some people prefer kissing with their eyes opened, reasoning that gazing into their partner's eyes makes the kiss more intense, or they want to see the effect they are having on their partner. "Wide-eyed" kissing has some drawbacks, though. Your partner looks like a cyclops unless you're willing to endure the necessary eye strain to keep focus. And if one of you chooses to close your eyes, the other is left gazing into a pair of eyelids. Unless the two of you are myopic, the easier solution is for everyone simply to kiss with closed eyes.

Kissing with the eyes closed creates another kissable facial surface —the eyelid. While many people enjoy the sensation, it poses a problem for contact-lens wearers because the pressure on the lens is painful. And women who wear eye make-up don't want it smeared across the rest of their face.

EARS

The ears can be a wonderful stimulation point in a kiss because of their sensitivity. However, far too often they get abused by people speaking too loud, blowing too hard, or planting a kiss so wet that it sends the recipient sprinting for a Q-tip. Unless your partner is hard of hearing, you should never speak directly into an ear. Whispering is great because it sends small short bursts of air directly into the recipient's ear, creating tickling and/or shivering sensations that most find stimulating and enjoyable.

Blowing deliberately into someone's ear is a very popular, though tricky form of seduction. Never form a seal between lips and ear or you can cause significant inner-ear damage. Blowing should be light and sustained, as if you're blowing on hot soup or coffee. And never blow into someone's ear if you have something in your mouth.

If you want to use your tongue for added excitement around the ear, for goodness sake, don't drivel. Drenching someone's ear is a major kissing faux pas. The suction technique described earlier will prevent any saliva buildup, as will pausing to swallow.

Try lightly nibbling on your partner's earlobes, tracing the ear with your nose, or lightly touching all over the ear using one of your fingers. Remember that any noise close to the ears will be greatly magnified (humming could sound like an air raid alert), so keep all sounds to a minimum.

Inhaling is an appealing alternative to blowing into your partner's ear. Put your lips near the ear and lightly inhale through your mouth the same way you suck on a straw.

If you treat the ears properly during a kiss, you can heighten the experience. And don't linger on the ear for too long. It's like force-feeding cheesecake; too much of a good thing diminishes its value, but a little taste leaves you hungry for more.

HEIGHT

It is more common for kissing partners to be of unequal heights so for most of us, a standing kiss will require that one head falls back and the other forward. With the average head weighing eight to ten pounds, holding this position is a significant strain on the neck.

In the event that you're not quite ready to get horizontal, try finding a kissing position that reduces the height delta. Have the taller partner sit or lean on something, or have the shorter one find a stair or high-heeled shoes to stand on. Or try sitting down.

HANDS

The hands rule is: "If it's traditionally covered by underwear, don't touch it." Now, if the two of you are very familiar with one another, this rule certainly need not apply. But generally speaking, a kiss can be ruined if hands navigate their way onto controversial body parts. The conservative approach is always to keep your hands above your partner's neck or around the waist.

For those of you with a more southerly final destination in mind, there is an acceptable alternative for your hands. Start touching a neutral area, then when the two of you become comfortable kissing, slowly begin moving one hand toward your goal. This signals your partner of your eventual target.

If you're on the receiving end and do not like where your partner's hands are heading, stay calm and continue kissing, but lightly take the guilty hand and move it somewhere more appropriate. You may have to repeat this, but after a few times, he or she should get the picture. If your partner continues groping, take more aggressive action, such as leaving.

Once the hands are situated satisfactorily, focus on hand movement. The person in your arms wants to be caressed. Gently touch and stroke him or her in an affectionate manner. Tickling, poking, and quick darting movements are inappropriate and unappealing, as is focusing on one spot and rubbing it till the skin becomes raw or desensitized. The hands should continually search out new areas, keeping your partner alert and aroused, and forcing you to be creative.

NOSE

The nose is the greatest barrier to a kiss on the lips. Often times we find ourselves head-tilting from side to side trying to settle in for a kiss. Though this nose juking is frustrating, most people instinctively tilt to the right. So from now on, let's all tilt to the right and eventually the nose crash problem will disappear.

Be alert to the location of your partner's nose, making certain that it's not obstructed or squashed. Kissing and rubbing noses is a perfectly acceptable practice. Exploring the insides of the nose with your tongue, or trying to bite nose hairs is a definite no-no. And don't even think about kissing if you have a runny nose. Your partner could catch your cold (or your run-off).

BREATHING

Do it. For whatever reason, some prefer to refrain from breathing during a kiss. This causes lightheadedness and increases saliva production. Breathing lets you kiss longer without having to break for air. Try breathing lightly through your nose, or learn to pull back to light lip touching so you can catch some air.

Be sensitive to your partner's breathing as well. If your partner breaks away from your kiss gasping for air, chances are your kissing obstructs his or her breathing. Also, if your partner is breathing through the mouth, you're probably guilty of nose-smashing. Be especially alert if you're kissing an asthmatic. These people have a hard time breathing even when not being kissed. Take extra precautions to give them some room.

VARIATION

A woman once confided in me that she had been kissed by a human typewriter. Beginning at the left ear, he planted a row of kisses over to her right ear, then, at the imaginary ring of the carriage return, he shot back to the left ear and started all over again.

Kissing should never be a programmed set of movements. It should be spontaneous and unpredictable. Repeated lip-to-lip kissing becomes boring, and can cause lip chapping. Try lip nibbles, tongue whips, nose brushes, or any other creative modifications you can come up with. (See page 112, "A List of Kisses.") Varying your kisses keeps your partner attentive and can make the kissing last longer.

TIMING

Don't prolong a kiss if your partner wants to stop. Ending a kiss while you both want more is safer than suffering the embarrassment of having your partner ask you to get off his or her face. Likewise, don't launch into a passionate kiss at the very beginning. It can set your partner on the defense, or worse, can turn him or her off completely. Let the intensity and duration of your kisses grow until the time feels appropriate to move on to more involved kissing.

POSITION

The key is finding a position that doesn't cause limbs to fall asleep or muscles to stretch into unnatural postures. Allow enough distance between you to prevent the compression of body parts, but not so much space that it is difficult to touch the lips. Avoid kissing with an obstacle between the two of you, such as a fence, table, or stick shift of a car. It is also bad form to force your partner on to his or her back first.

Have fun experimenting to find new and creative kissing positions. (See page 122, "Kissing Embraces.")

STRENGTH

Men generally are stronger than women, so a woman can be easily frightened when a man is too physical. Men should never pin a woman down, constrain her movements, or put her in a hold that she can't easily break out of. It is the man's responsibility to make certain that the woman always feels safe and secure in his company.

These are the basic elements of a well-executed kiss. It is important that you make a careful and honest evaluation of each element to identify any shortcomings in your kissing technique. Once the errors are corrected and the proper method put to practice, the next step is to develop a kissing style unique to your own personality.

♥

KISSING ETIQUETTE

♥

In spite of its common practice, kissing never seems to go smoothly. Noses bump, lips miss, make-up smears, and earrings fly.

Avoiding a kiss may be just as clumsy and is usually more unpleasant. You're forced to kiss homely relatives you've never met before, and as for the "goodnight" kiss" from someone you never want to see again, you'll close your eyes and turn a cheek or take it on tightly sealed lips. Is there any escape?

Help has finally arrived. These six basic points of kissing etiquette make up the Code of Kissing Courtesy, which will help you feel more comfortable about kissing, and show you how to put your partner at ease.

Keep the Code with you at all times, and your conduct will stay on the right course during a kiss (romantic and otherwise).

♥

Don't Kiss and Tell This is the first and oldest rule of kissing as well as the one most often broken. Giving your friends a long and much embellished description of a kiss shows thoughtlessness toward your partner. Don't advertise.

Don't Over-kiss In the stock market, if you issue too many shares, you diminish each share's value. The same holds true of kisses. Stop short. It will almost certainly leave your partner wanting more; and win you a future opportunity to kiss.

Don't Kiss if You're Infectious If you're not feeling well, have a cold, mononucleosis, an open sore, or any other infectious condition, for heaven's sake, warn your partner and refrain from kissing.

Don't Laugh After a Kiss It's disturbing to hear a partner break into laughter immediately after a serious kiss. It can hurt feelings and break a romantic mood.

Don't Kiss Unless You Want to Kiss someone because you want to, not because you feel obligated. Giving a kiss out of pity, compensation for buying dinner, or merely to end an evening quickly are all poor reasons to kiss; you mislead the recipient. If you feel you must do something, that's what cards, flowers, and telephones are for.

Don't Kiss and Grope Are you kissing just to kiss, or kissing as a prelude to something else? If you're "just kissing," then your hands shouldn't be taking an inventory of your partner's body parts. Groping hands not only distract and presume, they're annoying.

❤

Some common kissing situations or circumstances baffle us. Here are recommendations on how to best handle them:

The Mouth or the Cheek? Kissing on the mouth should be reserved for spouses, lovers, close family members, and very, very close friends. Otherwise, it's best to kiss the cheek.

Hand Kissing Hand kissing, though popular in Europe, is not commonly practiced in America. Regardless, some hand kissing faux pas can be avoided. One should not kiss the hand of an unmarried woman. The lips shouldn't actually touch the skin. Finally, don't kiss the palm of a lady's hand; this sends all the wrong signals.

If the woman wants her hand kissed, she should extend her hand slightly higher than she would to receive a handshake with the palm down rather than open. A man who is not used to this gesture is better off shaking the woman's hand lightly than attempting to kiss it.

Kissing Babies
It's rude to kiss someone else's infant without permission. If you do, at least make sure it's a quick germ-free kiss.

Children and Kissing
Children should kiss only the people they really like, and they should not be forced to kiss anyone else. It's better to encourage your child to hug or extend a hand for a handshake.

Kissing Family Members
Some family members *love* to kiss each other, even when only a few hours may have elapsed between visits. Others never kiss, or only kiss after a *very* long absence. Regional variations, family background, and lineage make it hard to establish rules or guidelines.

Woman-to-Woman Kissing
One woman kissing another as a greeting seems commonplace these days. The elder of the two decides whether to kiss or shake hands (if you know which one that is). If the age difference is negligible, either party can initiate. Women usually head for the cheek and simulate any number of kissing gestures and sounds to avoid smearing lipstick.

Man-to-Man Kissing
Magic and Isiah do it; European men have been kissing cheeks for generations. Most American men, however, prefer a handshake or a hug.

Kissing in Public   The taboo on public kissing has relaxed over the last twenty-five years. Nevertheless, public kissing should be short and sweet. Aerobic tongue work and probing hands are public kissing no-no's. When amour strikes in public, find a private spot.

Kissing at Airports   Airports or other ports of call like train and bus stations send emotions racing more than other public places because people are either parting or reuniting. A short, sweet kiss usually won't satisfy the moment.

Get your leave-taking done in the car. If you insist on staying together until the final boarding call, at least find a semiprivate spot away from the crowd to kiss, and keep it brief. If someone is arriving, try to hold off until you reach the car before giving a passionate welcome or at least move out of the way of those who are trying to deboard.

The Goodnight Kiss   This is the most awkward kiss. Men feel obligated to attempt it; women feel obligated to comply.

Most of us dispense goodnight kisses as a ritual, or strictly out of habit. The goodnight kiss should never be the first romantic kiss between the two of you because it signals the end of the evening!

Do not worry about a goodnight kiss. You can always skip it, thank the other sincerely, and then say goodnight.

Kissing at the Front Door   Let's assume your evening went well, that proper etiquette reigned, and the two of you now stand at the front door. The general front door rule is to keep the kiss short. Men, don't linger around like a cat waiting to be let in afterwards.

Clothing   Loosely woven garments can snag while fashions with tassels, beads, and other accoutrements can get caught or even blind your partner. Also be wary of soft knits that may be allergens.

Jewelry Men think twice about moving in on protruding pins and sharp earrings that can skin noses, scratch skin, or tear clothing. Men: Watch your watch. It can catch and get tangled in hair or clothing.

Eye Glasses For the record, men *do* make passes at women who wear glasses, and vice versa. Anyway, 20/20 vision isn't necessary for great kissing because most of us kiss with our eyes closed.

Glasses only become a kissing issue when both of you wear them. You need to work together to find the right position to prevent eyewear from crashing, or you could both take off your glasses.

Glasses can even become a great prop for kissing. Remove your partner's glasses gently and seductively to signal that a kiss is on its way. If you wear glasses, remove them as a gesture of willingness.

Gum If you're caught with gum in your mouth, you have two choices: discreetly remove it, or swallow it.

Breath Mints Timing is everything. You can look presumptuous popping a mint in your mouth seconds before moving in for a kiss, or excusing yourself only to come back with Binaca breath. Chew breath mints after you eat something pungent, then politely offer one to your partner as well. Don't try to hide the fact that you've taken one.

Regional Variations Kissing customs vary from one region to the next in this great country. People from large cities are more accustomed to social kissing. Those from Washington, D.C., New Yorkers, Californians, and Southerners often greet their most casual acquaintances with kisses. Midwesterners and Westerners tend to be reserved, indulging far less in social kissing.

Kissing Around the World   Be aware that many countries have quite different attitudes and responses toward kissing. Here's a sample list:

FRENCHMEN will kiss you twice—once on each cheek or three times in some regions.

BELGIANS often kiss you three times.

CHINESE, for the most part, do not kiss in public.

WEST AFRICANS feel repulsed to see tourists kissing.

AUSTRIANS are famous for kissing on the hand.

INDONESIANS kiss only the cheek.

LAPLANDERS may kiss the mouth and the nose at the same time.

JAPANESE, before their contact with the West, did not practice kissing.

GERMANS have thirty words for kissing; for example, *Nachkuss* is a kiss given to make up for kisses that were overlooked.

GREEKS like to kiss hello on the mouth; even male friends do it.

FINLANDERS consider mouth-to-mouth kissing obscene.

ARAPESHIANS, according to Margaret Mead, touch lips together and draw each other's breath in.

ESKIMOS, MALAYSIANS, POLYNESIANS, BALINESE primarily rub noses.

INDIA recently lifted a ban on actual mouth contact in movies.

ARABS AND HINDUS consider kissing an erotic act.

♥

TURN-ONS AND TURN-OFFS

♥

Here is a general listing of kissing turn-ons and turn-offs, though people have different quirks and preferences.

KISSING TURN-ONS

TONGUE, since most people like deep kissing
EYES CLOSED
PERFUME
LIPSTICK, an exciting status symbol for some men
SUSPENSE, causing pleasant excitement in anticipation of the eventual kiss
TENDERNESS
A SLOW BUILD, or being charmed into a kiss
CANDLELIGHT
SOFT VOICE, whispering, or speaking softly near the ear
SPONTANEITY
TONGUE SUCKING, having your tongue lightly sucked by your partner
CONFIDENCE
HEARING THE OTHER'S BREATHING, especially if it becomes short and excited
SIGHS AND MOANS
FACIAL HAIR, women either love it or hate it
LIGHT NIBBLING
PASSION, the kind that makes you feel you're the object of desire
THE POSSIBILITY OF GETTING CAUGHT
MUSIC

MOISTURE, a kiss that's a little on the wet side
DARKNESS
THE WOMAN MAKING THE FIRST MOVE
KISSING FOREPLAY, or touching before actually kissing
CARESSING
EMOTIONAL INVOLVEMENT

KISSING TURN-OFFS

BAD BREATH (see page 89, "Breathless Kissing")
WRONG BODY POSITION, one that feels awkward, uncomfortable,
   or inappropriate
FACIAL HAIR STUBBLE
SEVERE TONGUE SUCKING, or sucking your partner's tongue with
   too much force
EYES OPEN
LEAP-FROGGING, or an illogical succession of kisses (kissing the forehead,
   moving to the knee cap, back up to the eyes, over to the hand, and
   then down to the toes)
STARTING A KISS WITH THE MOUTH OPEN TOO WIDE
BITING
NO PARTICIPATION FROM PARTNER
BAD TONGUE MOVEMENT
KISSES THAT ARE TOO WET
LIPSTICK, since most adult men do not care for lipstick
COLD OR SWEATY HANDS
TOO MUCH LIP PRESSURE
LIFELESS LIPS
SMOKING
TIGHTLY PURSED LIPS
SOMETHING OFFENSIVE IN THE MOUTH prior to the kiss
   (liver, gas siphon, chewing tobacco)

EARLIER LOCATION OF THE HANDS (in dirt, touching diapers, in the nose)
KISSING THE PET, THEN YOU
PICKING TEETH
FALSE TEETH
AWKWARDNESS
TONGUE TOO FAR DOWN THE OTHER'S THROAT
TOO MUCH TALKING
HAVING THEIR EYES KISSED, FOR CONTACT LENS WEARERS AND WOMEN WHO WEAR EYE MAKEUP
GROPING
RUSHING (or failing to perform) the preliminaries
HANDS IN THE HAIR of a man who is going bald, or of a woman who has spent a lot of time putting it in place
KISSING IN PUBLIC
CHAPPED LIPS
DRY, ROUGH SKIN
BODY ODOR

❤ DEEP KISSONYMS ❤

FRENCHING	SPIT SWAPPING	TONGUE TALK
HOT TONGUING	SWAPPING SPIT	TONGUE TO TONGUE
LIP SUSHI	SWEETY SMOOCH	TONGUE WRESTLING
MARAICHINAGE	TASTE BUD DINNER	TONGUE TUMBLE
JOWL SUCKING	TASTE BUD THRUST	TONSIL DIVING
SOUL KISS	TASTE BUD PROJECTILE	TONSIL SWABBING
SPIN CYCLE	TONGUE DANCING	TONSIL SWALLOWING
SPIT SAMPLING	TONGUE SANDWICH	

BREATHLESS KISSING

♥

Halitosis has become a phobia because there's no absolute way of knowing whether your breath is offensive. Don't worry about dashing off for a quick gargle; you can now breathe easier. Here is the lowdown on primary causes of bad breath and solutions for preventing it.

CAUSES

Food Particles Bacteria live off the bits of food left in the mouth after eating. The longer the food debris sits, the more potent the stench.

Sulfur Eating foods with a high sulfur content is a breath wrecker. When these foods are digested, the sulfur-containing compounds get into the bloodstream, which eventually works its way into the lungs. In two to four hours the result becomes the unpleasant smell referred to as "dog breath." It can take up to twenty-four hours to clear out of your system.

Foods high in sulfur include: garlic, fish, horseradish, cabbage, onions, eggs, broccoli, brussels sprouts, coffee, red meat, and red hot peppers. Cooking these foods, in some cases, can help reduce their effect on the breath. Eating parsley as an antidote is just a myth.

Pyrazine This is another compound that can give a peculiar, though not necessarily bad odor to the breath. It is found in nuts, coffee, chocolate, asparagus, green bell peppers, potato and corn chips, bacon flavoring, and foods claiming a "roasted" flavor.

Alcohol Beer, wine, and hard liquor have a distinctive aroma that gets into the bloodstream, only to show up a few hours later as a fruity, unpleasant breath odor.

Some alcoholic beverages create a more potent breath odor than others because of the way they are made. Beer is brewed with hops, scotch is made with barley, and wine can be aged in oak barrels, all of which give the breath a stronger odor than, say, vodka, which is normally distilled from bland potatoes. Boozy breath can last up to twenty-four hours.

Smoking Cigarette, cigar, and pipe smoking guarantee bad breath. The smoke permeates not only the tissues of the mouth but also the hair, skin, and clothing. Smoker's breath lasts up to seventy-two hours after smoking.

High Protein Diet Diets that include very little or no carbohydrates put the body in a state of ketosis, thereby giving the breath an unpleasant acetone scent. (This type of diet also makes for unpleasant body odor.)

Dehydration Medications that dehydrate the body, such as antihistamines and motion-sickness pills, can cause foul-smelling breath. A solution is to drink fluids to rehydrate the body.

Stress and exercise interrupt normal breathing and swallowing patterns, consequently reducing mouth moisture. If you notice a sour taste or a sticky feeling in your mouth, it should be a tip-off that your breath is uncertain. Chewing gum or eating food will help speed the rehydration process.

Sleep "Morning breath" is simply dryness of the mouth. Saliva is a built-in breath freshener, continually cleaning and rinsing. However, when we sleep so do our salivary glands. (We swallow only twenty times during an average night's sleep versus 2,000 times during the waking hours.) Snoring and open-mouthed breathing make the problem worse by further drying the mouth.

Morning breath is easily rectified by eating or drinking something to re-stimulate the salivary glands. A citrus juice is especially effective. Tartness jump-starts saliva flow into action.

Menstrual Cycle Breath odor can occur for women around the time of ovulation. An increased level of estrogen triggers shedding of soft tissues throughout a woman's body, including mouth tissue, giving mouth bacteria more debris to feed on.

Gum Disease Gum disease creates extremely offensive breath odor owing to the decomposing bacteria that collect in pockets around the teeth. A good oral hygiene program can eliminate the problem.

Health problems Diabetes and kidney failure carry distinctive and very unpleasant breath odors. Ulcers or respiratory problems can also cause breath odor. In fact, foul breath can signal a nose, mouth, or throat infection. Any strong or unusual breath scent should be a tip-off to see a doctor.

SOLUTIONS

Since there are many causes, there is no one cure for bad breath. Breath odor comes from both the mouth and the lungs, and the primary culprit, mouth bacteria, can't and shouldn't be completely removed owing to their role in digestion.

There are temporary solutions to the problem, however.

Gums, Mints, Drops, and Sprays These are designed to mask breath odor. They do not remove trapped food particles, and only slightly stimulate saliva output. Some mints contain copper, which will temporarily neutralize the smell caused by sulfurous foods. Basically these products disguise foul breath for no more than ten to fifteen minutes, with drops and sprays lasting the longest because of their concentration.

Be sure these products are sugarless, because sugar requires digestion and therefore attracts more bacteria, as do the artificial sweeteners mannitol and sorbitol. The best breath sugar substitute reportedly is xylitol.

Mouthwashes Mouthwashes are more effective because they swish away some food particles, kill some bacteria, mask some odors, and can last up to two hours. However, they are still only a temporary cure.

Effective mouthwashes fall into two categories: (1) those that neutralize sulfur smells with zinc chloride (mostly found in red mouthwashes); and (2) those that go after bacteria. Two ingredients to look for are domiphen bromide and cetylpyridinium chloride (usually found in yellow and green mouthwashes).

Brushing Brushing, along with flossing, is the best remedy for bad breath. What most people don't realize is that the tongue needs to be brushed as well if brushing is going to have any significant impact on your breath.

A study by professor Joseph Tonzetich, Ph.D., in the School of Dentistry at the University of British Columbia in Vancouver found that brushing the tongue is the single most effective method of decreasing breath odor.

DETECTING BAD BREATH

Here are three techniques that can be used to detect and locate the source of breath odor.

1 Lick the back of your hand, wait a minute, then sniff. If odor-producing bacteria are at work in your mouth, there will be a decidedly sour odor.
2 Cup your hands and breathe out through the mouth and then in through the nose. Normal breath has a slightly sweetish scent.
3 Find a *good* friend. Hold your breath and have the person sniff the inside of your mouth to see if it is the source of the odor. Next, breathe through your mouth. If the friend detects a bad odor, it's coming from the lungs. Finally, close your mouth and breath through your nose. If your breath smells, you may have a sinus infection.

The good news about halitosis is that we worry about it more than we need to. One expert on oral hygiene products estimates that only 1 person in 100 has noticeable bad breath without using a breath enhancer. Remember also that bad breath is in the nose of the beholder. It depends on what you're used to; Italians don't mind garlic, Indonesians don't mind curry, and dogs don't mind dog breath. Persistent, pernicious bad breath, of course, should be looked into by a dentist.

BAD BREATH SYNONYMS

DINOSAUR BREATH	ITALIAN PERFUME
BRONX VANILLA	NOSE NUKER
DOG BREATH	ONE-ORDER-OF-FRIED-ONIONS
GUTTER BREATH	SKUNK BREATH
HALITOSIS	TEARJERKER

mastering
the Art

♥

EXTRAORDINARY KISSING

♥

It is rumored that musicians who play woodwind or brass instruments are the best kissers because of their highly developed lip muscles. Though this theory merits some consideration, tuba lessons alone won't turn you into an outstanding kisser.

Being extraordinary means going beyond what is usual, customary, or required. Many musicians, for instance, are technically competent, yet what leads one to outperform another is his or her ability to go beyond mere proficiency. Emotional involvement, sensitivity, and a respect for the music and the instrument set the stars apart. Great kissing requires more than technical accuracy. Six qualities are essential.

IMAGINATION

What gives kissing surprise, excitement, and intrigue is imagination. If you think you're not imaginative, you're wrong: You fill out your income tax form, improve fish stories, and entertain yourself. Being imaginative also means being resourceful. The next time you watch television, read a romantic novel, or go to the movies, be open to ideas for your next kiss. Try creating kisses that belong exclusively to you and your partner. Kiss your partner so he or she responds with an "ooh," an "aah," and a quickened pulse. Develop a way to send kisses through the telephone. A distinctive kiss not only shows imagination but sends your partner the signal that he or she is special and different from anyone else.

EXPERIMENTATION

Grasping the qualities that give your partner the greatest pleasure and enhancing them with a new style and expression is what extraordinary kissing is all about. Experimenting helps you find these qualities.

Try using different embraces, kissing places other than the lips, or varying the intensity of your kisses, paying attention to your partner's responses so you'll discover his or her preferences.

Kissing games such as spin the bottle, post office, name that kiss, bobbing for tongues, and king of the mouth provide a good medium for experimentation. Send messages to your partner in kissing Morse code, or tongue wrestle.

Kissing games can center on food. Have a food fight between mouths. Or try sharing something like licorice, starting at the same time but at opposite ends. Have you ever played mouth hockey? Start with an M&M held between the tips of your tongues. The goal is the back of your partner's mouth. The game begins after the third nose rub, and ends when either the M&M dissolves or one of you eats it.

Kissing experimentation ought to be an ongoing practice. With a little creativity, your kisses will never be boring.

KINDNESS

Kissing with kindness is like eating with manners. It is easier to kiss a person who shows kindness than someone who tries to slam dunk you onto a couch before learning your name.

Follow the Golden Rule. Do unto others as you would have others do unto you, and you'll help the person you're with feel more comfortable. You'll also show by example how you want to be treated. For example:

1 Have you made sure your partner is comfortable before beginning to kiss?

2 Is your partner relaxed (and not just drunk)?
3 Do you make an effort to detect what kind of kissing your partner likes?
4 Would you like to be kissed the way you're kissing your partner?
5 If asked, would your partner say you are tender and gentle?

If you answered no to any one of these questions, you haven't been entirely kind.

When the two of you operate on the same "kindness wavelength," your kissing naturally becomes extraordinary. Kindness should also be mutual, otherwise you need to rethink the person and the situation.

CONFIDENCE

Confident kissing carries the conviction that, no matter what happens, you can manage any kissing situation. If your first attempt at a kiss doesn't work, regroup and try a different approach. Have faith in your skills.

If you've had poor aim, suffered criticism, or been deserted in the past, learn from your mistakes and then recognize that they're history. Future partners will know nothing about your past kissing traumas. It's one of the few opportunities in life where you get a fresh start.

Confident kissing takes time. First you must overcome kissing worries: How far will it go? How will your partner react—laugh? pant? yawn? How will you perform? If or when should you use your tongue? Is your breath okay? Remember that there's no one magical, sure-fire way to kiss anyone. The two of you are in the same boat: neither has kissed the other before. Like running on a treadmill, worrying gets you all worked up, but it doesn't get you anywhere.

Realize that no one's clocking your trip to first base, and a kiss does not have to take place before concluding the first date, or the second, or the third. Take your time, and become familiar with the other person. It's comforting and can strengthen your confidence.

Don't think about all the things that might go wrong. Instead, look forward to kissing.

Do a little research. Discover your date's favorite music, sports, his or her alma mater. Familiarity strengthens confidence. Just remember that the line between self-confidence and conceit is a fine one. Be open to the possibility that your kissing can always stand improvement.

COMMUNICATION

That our lips are designed to form kisses, as well as words, gives proof positive that the two should always go hand-in-hand.

Without conversation, a kiss can be misconstrued. Suppose your partner kisses you ambiguously during a first date, then goes on to recall something completely irrevelant. Was it done out of obligation, or affection? Or was it merely an experiment? And if so, how did you rate? You will probably spend a good deal of time running the scenario by your best friends for their interpretation. Such needless wondering can be eliminated by communicating.

Conversing with your partner also uncovers your partner's kissing preferences. Even one word ("Wow") after a kiss announces your partner's enthusiasm. Dialogue on other topics helps you gain insights into your partner, which help you feel more comfortable and perhaps less vulnerable. Conversation makes each kiss better than the one before.

You can also communicate with your partner through notes, cards, letters, a video, a poem, or a riddle. Or get your message across with some unusual communication means like charades, a Pictionary game, a palm reader (with a previously well-greased palm), an impersonator, Western Union, or even David Letterman's viewer mail. Sharing more thoughts with your partner can only make the kisses between you better. Howl like dogs if you want; just communicate.

Good communication is as stimulating as black coffee, and just as hard to sleep after. The same can be said of a good kiss. Enjoy communicating and kissing, and worry about sleeping later.

RESPECT

Respecting the person you kiss means you find that person valuable and worthy of special treatment. Mutual respect neutralizes many of our unattractive tendencies and forces our motives to be honorable. When you respect someone, you show your best side; you want to please, and you pay attention. You may be showing a lack of respect for your partner without realizing it. Ask yourself these questions:

1 Have you ever kissed someone you didn't care for?
2 Have you ever kissed to get something you wanted?
3 Have you ever kissed just to make another person jealous?
4 Have you ever used a kiss to lead someone on?
5 Have you ever used a kiss as a weapon?
6 Have you ever kissed someone out of guilt or obligation?

A yes to any one of these questions shows you weren't respecting your partner. If you don't care for someone, don't kiss them. By refusing to kiss indiscriminately, you increase the value of your kisses.

You may be showing respect, but not getting it in return. Put yourself in your partner's shoes and see if you're stepping on toes. Pay attention to timing. A kiss shortly after a first meeting is a red flag; holding off gives time for you to develop regard and admiration for each other.

Take things slowly, one step at a time. Don't skip hand holding and hugging. When the kiss finally happens, it will be fabulous.

Now that you know what it takes to be extraordinary, go for it! Kiss with imagination, experimentation, kindness, confidence, communication, and respect and outstanding results are almost guaranteed.

❤

OPINIONS FROM THE EXPERTS

❤

What do the pros think? I surveyed fifty individuals who were referenced by others as exceptional kissers. Their answers constitute this section.

TO SEE OR NOT TO SEE

❤ Most people prefer kissing with their eyes closed, though some switch, opening their eyes occasionally (or for certain occasions). Very few people kiss with eyes open, and the majority who do are men.

❤ Advocates of closed eyes claim "it sets a better mood," and "it allows for more imagination." Moreover, "you have no distractions so you can concentrate on what you're doing." "It just feels sexier."

❤ As for those who straddle the fence, they say, "Close your eyes when you're kissing on the lips because you're too close to focus. Otherwise, open your eyes so you can hit what you're aiming at." They also made the point that you need not close your eyes for a social or friendly kiss, though it's appropriate to do so for intimacy.

❤ The few who argued for open eyes insisted that it's more sensual and more intense. On a practical note, they like to see the effect they're having on their partner.

TO BEARD OR NOT TO BEARD

❤ Most women don't like to kiss men with facial hair for reasons of cleanliness and pain—"It hurts!" Most men have heard, and sympathize with their complaints.

ON LIPSTICK TRACES

❤ For the most part, men do not like lipstick, claiming, "It's for decoration only; it does nothing to enhance the kiss." It does, however, increase dry-cleaning bills, they complained. "If it's very light, then it's all right," said some, while others agreed that "painted lips are great to look at; clean, fresh lips are perfect for kissing."

❤ Most women advise: "Don't wear lipstick if you want to be kissed." One woman even suffered the embarrassment of having a man offer her a handkerchief to remove her lipstick. Of course, "just the right amount, worn properly, can invite a kiss."

A KISS IS JUST A KISS BUT
SOME KISSES ARE BETTER THAN OTHERS

Here's what the experts had to say about their most memorable kisses:

❤ "My first kiss was the first time I ever experienced that nervous, excited feeling that goes down from your lips, pushing your stomach onto the floor."

❤ "We 'made eyes' at each other for a while, then had a long, slow-motion start. Our mouths barely opened, and our tongues just barely touched."

❤ "Once, I was truly taken by surprise. I experienced the most powerful kiss, I was really shaken up. For about an hour. I can't even describe it—you had to be there."

❤ "He started very slowly and softly, and miraculously knew just when and how to build up the tempo and the passion until he literally left me breathless."

❤ "My best kiss was with a twenty-one-year-old blond who was convinced she would go to hell for kissing a married man, but wanted to anyway."

- "It happened in the middle of a conversation. We'd kiss. We'd talk. We'd kiss some more, then talk some more. Eventually, we were just kissing."
- "My best kisses have always come after my best margaritas."
- "When I was in the seventh grade, I experienced my first 'French kiss'—with an older woman. [She was 13.] I think it was nerves, or the anticipation, or the thrill of doing something for the *first time*. I still think about it twenty years later."
- "I was in my father's car, and I left the motor running while we kissed goodnight. I went through half a tank of gas."

MEMORABLE KISSES YOU'D RATHER FORGET

- Both men and women vividly recall "limp and lifeless tongues," and being slobbered by people who had large mouths or too much to drink. One woman even claims to have had her waterproof mascara licked off. Then, of course, there's stubble burn.
- Men spoke of times when they were young and inexperienced— before they knew what went where. One had even been laughed at (and it wasn't his fault).
- Nobody likes kissing without participation from his or her partner.

HOW DO YOU LIKE TO BE HELD?

"I don't," responded one gentleman. "I like to focus on the kiss and minimize other sensations."

Men like to be held gently, and they enjoy having fingers run through their hair. Women, on the other hand, like to be held firmly—not too firmly, though. Everyone likes to be caressed, and lying down together is always nice.

WHAT ARE YOUR TRICKS OF THE TRADE?

When asked what makes them good kissers, the experts responded: spontaneity, natural ability, tenderness, sensitivity, and passion. Some were taught by great kissers, and others thoroughly enjoy it—and it shows. One man said simply, "I'm French. Need I say more?"

WHEN IS THE TIME RIGHT?

People are pretty ambiguous about timing. Most suggested, "you can see it in their eyes," "you can feel it," or "the mood is right." Otherwise, just kiss when you can't wait any longer.

WHEN ISN'T A KISS ROMANTIC?

When asked to describe their funniest, or most awkward kiss, the respondents had some colorful stories:

- ❤ "I opened my eyes to see if his were closed. To my horror, he was just staring at me."
- ❤ "I got a nosebleed in the middle of a very passionate kiss."
- ❤ "We were kissing, passionately, and I happened to have been standing on a mound of dirt (so I could reach him). I slipped, and he opened his eyes to find me staring at his zipper."
- ❤ "The slats on the bed broke. We fell to the floor, and woke everyone up with the crash."
- ❤ "I was once caught—in an airplane lavatory."
- ❤ "Once, when I was in high school, I went parking. My car sank into the mud during the two hours we kissed. I had to get it towed out."
- ❤ "As a bubblegum-chewing teenager, I kissed a girl with braces. It all happened so fast, but we were stuck together for quite some time."
- ❤ "I used to have a tooth in the roof of my mouth. (I've since had root canal to remove it.) A girl discovered it with her tongue. She leapt

back, turned white, and asked me what it was. I told her it was gum, and refused to kiss her anymore."

SOME POINTERS FROM THE PROS

The experts were asked to share their special techniques:

- ♥ To show that he's taken your breath away, one woman advises "pull away, catch your breath, and lightly moan after a kiss."
- ♥ "Gently run your tongue across the person's eyelids, and then across the brows," or "lick your partner's lips."
- ♥ Generally speaking, *relax*, be creative, be tender, take your time, and work your way up to a passionate kiss. It goes without saying that you should really care for the person you're kissing.
- ♥ Move to a rhythm . . . the rhythm is in your head; you don't have to hear it.
- ♥ As soon as you finish a kiss, lightly blow into your partner's mouth.
- ♥ If your partner is good at kissing—say so. People like to hear it.

WHEN SHOULD YOU KISS AND TELL?

The experts were asked if they could tell whether or not someone would be a good kisser (before kissing). Not one person felt that he or she could tell.

♥ HICKEY KISSONYMS ♥

HOOVER	STRAWBERRY KISS
KISS BITE	VAC ATTACK
MONKEY BITE	

♥

SOCIAL KISSING

♥

No one is safe from the unsolicited social kiss. It's showing up everywhere. Friendly gatherings, business functions, and, of course, parties have turned into battlegrounds laced with lip land mines that go off without warning. Even when it's acceptable to kiss socially, how do you perform this ambiguous kiss?

Social kissing has two categories: sociable kissing and business kissing. Sociable kissing occurs when you bump into a friend, or are at a gathering of personal friends and acquaintances. Business kissing includes kissing at business functions, or at gatherings with current or potential business associates.

SOCIABLE KISSING

Sociable kissing as a greeting has become very commonplace these days. This is unfortunate because too many of us feel that sociable kissing is meaningless, phony, or insincere. In addition to distrust, a wake of confusion and frustration surrounds the act; a sociable kiss, unlike a handshake, never seems to go smoothly. While you may aim for a cheek, the other may aim for a direct hit on the lips.

Kiss someone at a social gathering because you consider them very special—too good for a handshake or a nod. Don't kiss indiscriminately.

Often, more than one of your dearest friends will attend the same party. Do you kiss them all and risk being branded an insincere kisser? If you're kissing more than six people, you should stop and ask yourself what you're doing. Either you're everyone's best friend, or you're not being selective enough, thereby devaluing your kisses. It's smarter to err on the side of kissing too few people. Just remember that handshakes and hugs are gestures of greeting as well.

Here are a few guidelines to help you muddle through those social gatherings:

1 Between the two of you, the one deemed "more important" (ranking family member, host) has the right to initiate the kiss. If this distinction isn't obvious, the woman gets the right by default.

2 The woman chooses what to offer up for the kiss (lips, a cheek, or a hand); the man must oblige with one exception. If she offers her hand, the man has the option of either kissing or shaking it.

3 There is no penalty for not kissing. Here are three basic techniques for fending off unwanted on-coming sociable kissers:

❤ Quickly move forward and grasp the person's upper right arm (near the shoulder) with your left hand to neutralize the person. Then, grasp the right hand with yours in a warm handshake. The person is forced to comply.

❤ Offer your hand while keeping your arm rigid. If the person tries to come at you for a kiss, use your handclasp as leverage to hold the person off. If you're overpowered, give in, but turn a very "cold cheek."

❤ Take the person's hand in yours and cup it with your other hand. This gesture shows your warmth and that you like the person; at the same time it lets you escape the kiss.

4 If someone takes you by surprise with a kiss, don't show your annoyance or disgust. The person was wrong, but the whole incident will soon be forgotten.

Some social situations, in addition to friendly gatherings, automatically come with a sociable kissing permit. For example, when:

You greet your spouse.
Someone you like receives an honor or recognition.
You hear news that calls for congratulations.
Considerable time has passed since you've seen or spoken to the person.
You greet family and friends at celebrations or holidays.
Attending occasions of sadness or suffering, to show your sympathy and affection.
Receiving a gift.
Leaving for or returning from an adventure (lengthy trip, camp, boarding school, college, military service).

Sociable kissing may be on the rise, but that doesn't mean you have to participate. Kissing is a very powerful gesture. Use it honestly and selectively.

BUSINESS KISSING

Extending a hand used to be the *only* acceptable greeting in business, but now kissing has definitely arrived in the business world. It is on the increase, and in many cases it is replacing the handshake.

This swell in business puckering grew out of two trends: a continued blurring of the distinction between social and business etiquette, and an increase of women in the workplace.

There are a variety of opinions on this phenomenon. Some people feel business kissing is a social blunder unless the kissers are close friends outside the workplace. Others believe that kissing obscures the line and rank of command in a company, which lessens professionalism and credibility. Some people suggest it negatively accentuates gender differences. Sealing a business deal with a kiss has no legal grounds, and many compare it to giving to charity: once you start, you'll be expected to give every time you meet.

There are potentially two issues in business kissing: whether or not it's appropriate; and if so, how it should be executed. Here are just some variables to consider:

BUSINESS KISSING VARIABLES

CITY   _____
AGE   _____
RANK   _____
GENDER   _____
OCCASION   _____
LOCATION   _____
ONLOOKERS _____
PERSONAL RELATIONSHIP _____
PREVIOUS RELATIONSHIP _____

You must also take into account the industry in which you work, since every industry has its own culture.

KISS-HAPPY INDUSTRIES

FILM/MEDIA	HOTEL AND RESTAURANT	FINE ARTS
ADVERTISING	COSMETICS	APPAREL

NONKISSING INDUSTRIES

BANKING	MEDICINE	ENGINEERING
LAW	GOVERNMENT	MANUFACTURING
ACCOUNTING	INSURANCE	DATA PROCESSING

Should the occasion arise, here are the basics of business kissing to help you through this difficult and often awkward gesture:

1 A kiss on the lips in business is always inappropriate.
2 Lipstick marks should never be left.
3 Always let your superior be the one to initiate the kiss.
4 If a vigorous handshake will equally satisfy, don't kiss.
5 Don't play favorites and kiss only those you like best. Be consistent with your selection.
6 Don't kiss only those of a certain rank (just bosses, just subordinates).
7 Avoid kissing if either party has had alcohol. Sobriety is a must.
8 The spouse of an employee should not initiate a kiss.

If you're still not sure, it's safer not to risk a business kiss.

For those business associates you feel are worthy of more than the traditional handshake, there are alternative greetings that offer warmth without requiring that you take or give any lip:

1 **THE HALF HUG**   Shake right hands while you each put your left hand on the other's right upper arm or shoulder. This "almost" hug is acceptable in the office.
2 **THE HAND CUP SHAKE**   Join right hands, and cup the handshake with your left hand.
3 **THE HUG AND PAT**   A very loose hug leaves light between the two of you while you pat the other on the back.
4 **THE BACK PAT**   Approach the person from his or her left side, and pat the person on the back with your right hand. A handshake may immediately follow.

Kissing may be potentially abused in the business world, where everything can be exploited to someone's advantage. "Power Kissers" use kissing to leverage a better business position for themselves.

A power kiss is affectionless, but it makes some sort of power play. Recipients of power kisses should be aware that the gesture can be considered a put-down. A man might kiss a female business peer simply to send the message to others that he's the one who's really in charge. A woman who conspicuously offers up a cheek demanding an adoring peck, yet does not reciprocate, insinuates that the man is beneath her. Power kissing, if misconstrued, can become the makings of hot office gossip.

The victim of a power kiss can discourage future attempts by initiating the kiss and planting it on the cheek, or by avoiding the kiss altogether, intercepting it with a handshake.

Business kissing is an acceptable greeting in certain industries and situations, but be aware that you always take on some risk when you initiate even a harmless business kiss.

❤ MARATHON KISSONYMS ❤

BUNDLING	PROSPECTING	FOOL AROUND	SUBMARINE RACE
GIRAFFING	SMOOCHING	GIVE A HOT HOUSE	SUCK FACE
GRAZING	TURTLENECKING	GO INTO A HUDDLE	SWAPPIN' SPIT
LIP PUSH-UPS	APPLY THE ARMSTRONG	LIP MINGLING	TICKLIN' TONSILS
MOONTANNING	HEATERS	MAKING OUT	TONGUE TREKKING
MUGGING	ATTEND PARKOLOGY	MOLAR MASHING	TONGUE WRESTLE
NECKFEST	CATCHING MONK	MUG MUZZLE	WHOOPEE WARM-UP
NECKING	CHEW FACE	PETTING PARTY	
NUZZLING	EXPLORE THE WAISTS	PLAY POST OFFICE	
PETOLOGY	FLING WOO	SNOUT FRICTION	

♥

A LIST OF KISSES

♥

Even if it were your favorite food, if you were served something over and over again, eventually you'd welcome a change. Likewise, the same kiss again and again can become tedious and mechanical.

The following collection of kisses are the product of research, experience, and a little ingenuity.

SIMPLE KISSES

SIMPLE KISS   A lip-to-lip kiss with both parties applying light pressure.

KISSLET   A kiss where the lips barely touch.

PRESSURE KISS   A kiss with notable lip pressure.

PECK   A quick pressure kiss that concludes with a smacking lip sound.

PROLONGED KISS   A kiss sustained longer than is considered normal. The pressure during this kiss alternates between light and heavy.

CORNER KISS   Kissing the corners of the mouth, one at a time.

PRESSED KISS   A simple kiss with your partner's lower lip pressed between your two lips.

GREATLY PRESSED KISS   Holding your partner's lower lip between your two fingers, touch it with your tongue. Then replace your fingers with your lips and press his or her lower lip with force.

POUTING KISS   A kiss with your lips pouting.

KISS OF INNOCENCE   Standing a few feet apart and facing one another, the woman places her hands in his. Both close their eyes and lean forward until their lips meet in a kiss.

KNOB KISS A kiss with the lips overpuckered.

FISH KISS A kiss with "fish lips." (Separate your teeth and suck in your cheeks until the corners of your mouth meet.)

LIP LINK The man places a kiss on the woman's upper lip while the woman kisses the man's lower lip.

LIP-O-SUCTION The man lightly sucks the upper lip of the woman, while the woman lightly sucks the man's lower lip.

TULIPS (TWO LIPS) KISS A kiss with one partner's lips totally covering the other's lips.

CLASPING KISS A tulip kiss with sucking. The teeth should play no part in this kiss. (Those with facial hair may not find this kiss appealing.)

PALPITATING KISS A kiss where your lower lip moves in a pulsating fashion.

NIP KISS Blending a kiss with small cautious nibbles. Usually given on the lips, earlobes, neck, or cheeks.

113

HANDLE KISS You each take hold of the other's ears and draw them in close for a kiss. (Popular between adults and children.)

VACUUM KISS Barely touching your partner's lips with your own, draw in your breath. (This kiss is also given on the cheeks, neck, and other locations.)

LIGHT SWITCH KISS Kiss the upper lip and then immediately the lower lip of your partner. Also called the switch kiss.

MORSE CODE KISS Using long and short kisses, spell out messages to your partner in Morse code. (Note: both need to know Morse code—this is a great way to learn.)

DEEP KISSES

DEEP KISS A kiss where both parties have their lips parted, and the tongues explore and caress the inside of the other's mouth.

MILD MARAICHINAGE   A toned-down deep kiss where the tongues lightly touch and then withdraw.

FRENCH HUMMER   A deep kiss where one or both of you make humming sounds.

TONGUE TIP TANGO   With both tongues extended outside the mouth, each gently taps the tip of the other tongue.

TONGUE COMBAT   The tongues in playful battle with each other during a deep kiss.

TONGUE WRESTLE   While deep kissing, each of you tries to push the other's tongue back into its mouth.

SUCTION KISS   Creating suction during a deep kiss. (Suction is actively given by one partner and passively received by the other.)

BABY BOTTLE KISS   Draw your partner's tongue into your mouth and then lightly suck on it.

THE HOOVER   Form a tight seal between your lips and your partner's. Both of you then suck inward to create a vacuum inside your mouths. Reverse the suction before trying to separate, and do not hold this kiss for too long because it can become painful.

THE CLOSE SHAVE   Lightly hold your partner's tongue between your teeth while your partner moves his or her tongue back and forth. Your teeth will gently scrape or shave the tongue. A popular variation is to suck your partner's tongue into your mouth and then release it so your partner can pull it out.

LOOP KISS   Pass the tip of your tongue across your partner's upper lip and then along the lower lip. The movement creates a circle or a loop and can be done along the inner or outer side of the lips.

FRENCH EAR   Explore and caress the inside of your partner's ear with your tongue.

VOLLEY KISS   While deep kissing, the two of you alternate blowing into each other's mouths. The recipient's cheeks should expand.

BLAST SMACK   Each blows into the other's mouth during a deep kiss until the pressure becomes too great and forces the lips to break apart.

WIDE WORLD OF KISSES

WARM-UP KISSES   Kissing the nose, forehead, or cheek of your partner before kissing the mouth. (Also called the chaste kiss.)

BRUSH KISS   In a sweeping motion, your lips lightly brush the lips of your partner.

BROW BRUSH KISS   A brush kiss across the eyebrows.

CHEER-UP KISS   Usually given to a woman to cheer her up. While the woman is looking down at the ground, the man takes her chin in his hand and softly turns her face upward, then kisses her mouth.

MOVIE STAR KISS   Beginning at your partner's fingertips start a trail of kisses that eventually concludes with a dramatic kiss upon your partner's lips.

115

BUTTERFLY KISS   Flutter your eyelashes in place of your lips to kiss your partner. Popular butterfly kiss locations are the cheeks, lips, ears, and eyes. Also called the eyelash kiss.

TEASING KISS   Just before the two of you exchange a kiss, draw back and smile at your partner till you can stay away no more. Then slowly move in for the kiss.

ELECTRIC KISS   On a cool, dry night when the air is overloaded with electricity, the two of you shuffle your feet furiously on a carpet. When you both have a charge, lean over and slowly aim for each other's lips. With your lips about ½ inch apart, move in even slower until a spark jumps between the two of you. Instantly after this happens, kiss one another. You may have to practice this kiss several times in order to master it successfully. The natural reaction is to pull away. However, the pleasure is the kiss right after the shock. (If done in the dark, you'll see a spark.)

STOLEN KISS A stolen kiss is given fleetingly and spontaneously, taking the recipient by surprise. The initiator feigns disbelief of his or her own actions. Both parties must immediately move on after the exchange to eliminate the possibility of any further pursuit.

BACKSTAIRS KISS Similar to the stolen kiss, but more passionate, this is popular at parties or gatherings where guests can pretend to be tipsy or out of control. Most often performed in unusual locations such as behind a door or tree, or on the backstairs. The risk of being discovered in the act is the key element.

FINGER KISS First kiss your index finger. Then lightly touch your index finger to your partner's lips. (Can also be done using your three middle fingers.)

FINGERTIP KISS Kiss the tips of your partner's fingers in a fairly quick succession. (Make sure your kisses aren't too wet.)

PENDULUM KISS Your lips begin lightly touching one side of your partner's forehead, then brush softly across to the other side where you imprint a kiss. This kiss can also start at a corner of the mouth, lightly moving to the other corner to plant a kiss.

PROFILE KISS Place a series of light kisses along the profile of your partner's face. You may begin at the forehead or the chin. If you start at the forehead, conclude with a pressure kiss on the lips.

BROW KISS Use light nip kisses on the eyebrows. Make sure not to pull the brow hairs too hard.

TINGUIAN KISS Place your lips near your partner's face and suddenly inhale.

ESKIMO KISS Lightly rub your partner's nose with your own from side to side.

OCEANIC KISS Move your nose rapidly across your partner's face from one cheek to the other. Your noses should bump en route.

OLFACTORY KISS Place your nose near or against your partner's face then inhale through it. Also called the smell kiss.

19TH-CENTURY CHINESE-MONGOLIAN KISS Press your nose to your partner's cheek. Inhale through your nose and smack lips noisily.

LAPP KISS Kiss with your lips covering both the mouth and nose of your partner.

DOG KISS Generate short, quick breaths through your nose to imitate a dog sniffing. Then move your nose around the face and/or neck of your partner the same way a dog would.

PIG KISS Burrow your nose and mouth into the nape of your partner's neck and snort like a pig.

KISSY-FACE KISS Shower your partner's face with light kisses in quick succession.

CLOWN KISS The woman applies heavy lipstick to her lips and then kisses the man all over his face, leaving him with smeared lipstick marks.

ROSE GARDEN KISS The woman kisses the man over his entire body, leaving markings of where she's just kissed with tiny lipstick X's.

KISS À L'ORANGE Each of you place an orange quarter in your mouth, peel side showing, and then kiss.

TRAFFIC LIGHT KISS While stopped in a car at a traffic light, kiss your partner. (When the light changes, the kiss stops.)

THE WINDOW-WIPER Pass the tip of the tongue along your partner's upper lip from left to right and then from right to left. This kiss may also be given inside the mouth. The movement would be the same, but the tongue would instead move along the roof of the mouth.

NAPE KISS Lightly brush the lips up and down the back of the neck, which is an erogenous zone for many.

BACKBONE KISS A series of light kisses along the entire backbone, beginning just underneath the neck and traveling downward (at your own discretion).

LIMBO KISS Beginning just under the chin, the man showers light kisses down the woman's front until she stops him by touching his chin with her hand and pulling his lips up to hers for a kiss. (Named after the game of limbo where the challenge is to see how low you can go.)

FIGURE-EIGHT KISS Similar to the limbo kiss. The man kisses downward until the woman guides his head up so that she may kiss a trail down the man's front. He then guides her head back up and starts kissing downward again. The movement follows the shape of a figure eight.

TACKING KISS A series of kisses following a path that changes direction after each kiss. Named for the sailing term. Also known as the zigzag kiss.

THE CORTE Two pecks followed by two pressured kisses.

SOCIAL KISSES

SOCIAL KISS A kiss used as a gesture of greeting. An alternative to a handshake. (Usually on the cheek.)

AIR SMACK Approaching as if to kiss the cheek of the other, but instead making a noisy kiss in the open air near the cheek. The cheeks come very close, but do not touch.

DOUBLE AIR SMACK An air smack on each side.

SOCIALLY CONSERVATIVE SMACK While shaking right hands with your partner, lean forward, twisting your mouth as far to the left as possible, and lightly touch right jaws.

SIDESWIPE SMACK With the two of you standing side-by-side, brush the inside cheek while puckering your lips. (Sound is optional.)

OVER-THE-SHOULDER KISS Performed for the benefit of seeing who's behind the kissee, it is the gesture of the air smack without the noise. Also called "a mingling of perfumes."

GOLDFISH KISS   Also called the cheek-to-cheek kiss. With both parties holding their lips in a tight pucker, each brushes the cheek of the other without making a sound or spoiling any lipstick. A popular social kiss among women.

THE HUMMINGBIRD   With the mouth firmly closed, the kisser lightly touches the partner's cheek with his or her own while invoking a humming sound.

SOCIAL FRENCH KISS   A kiss commonly implemented by French officials. Grasping the upper arms of the other, place a pressure kiss on each cheek. Begin with the right cheek and then swing to the left one. Make sure the noses do not collide.

FRENCH-TO-FRENCH   A social French kiss with both parties participating in the kissing of the other's cheek. The two parties may perform this kiss either simultaneously or one can wait until the other is finished before beginning the kiss.

GROUP KISS   This kiss is used to acknowledge a group of people affectionately. The people closest to you receive air smacks or goldfish kisses. The people too far to reach are blown kisses.

KISS-THE-HAND   Man to woman. The man pretends to kiss the top side of the woman's hand, but his lips never actually touch.

TWO-HANDED LEAN   Walking forward with both hands outstretched, grab the two hands of your partner and form a circle. Each then leans into the circle and kisses the other on the lips or brushes the cheeks.

MISCELLANEOUS KISSES

GOOD MORNING KISS   The kiss given in the morning. Most of the time eyes are closed, aim is poor, and breath is bad.

MAKE-UP KISS   The kiss given when you feel sorry about something, or you know you should feel sorry about something.

BOO-BOO KISS   A kiss given to those places that have been hurt, cut, scraped, or bruised. Also called the first-aid kiss.

FROG KISS   A kiss given in the hope that when you open your eyes your partner will have transformed into a handsome prince or princess.

CANINE KISS   The kiss you get from your adoring dog. It's always wet, and always given affectionately.

CHICKEN KISS   The head darts forward and back in a split second, dispensing a quick peck with no lip.

FOREHEAD KISS   The kiss you get on your forehead from a person you're crazy for, though he or she knows you're too young.

LOOK-BOTH-WAYS KISS   A kiss given by people who don't like to be seen kissing so they will swing their head in both directions to see if anyone might be looking.

VAMPIRE KISS   A hickey on the neck.

SANDPAPER KISS   A kiss with an unshaven man.

EMORYBOARD KISS   A kiss with an unshaven woman.

TELEPHONE KISS   Simulating a kiss into the telephone receiver for the benefit of the person at the other end.

LETTER KISS   Kissing a letter and leaving lip prints. Lip print can be left using lipstick, grape juice, chocolate milk, inkpad—whatever.

TRAINING KISS   Any kiss to a mirror or pillow for the purpose of practicing kissing.

BLOWN KISS   Kiss your hand, then point it toward the kissee and blow. Used when the kissee is in close range.

THROWN KISS   Kiss your hands, then wave it in the kissee's direction. Used when the kissee is at a distance.

HURLED KISS   Rotate your upper body clockwise, and hold your hand to your mouth. Then unwind and extend your hand. Made popular on the TV show "The Dating Game." Used when the kissee is at a very far distance.

DIP KISS The man holds the woman in the dip dancing position, says something corny like "kiss me baby," then lays a mushy kiss on her.

This collection of kisses is in no way inclusive. Create your own by altering: touch ❤ pressure ❤ sound ❤ passion ❤ tongue ❤ nipping ❤ sucking ❤ brushing ❤ speed ❤ quantity ❤ lip position ❤ length

Working from the top on down, these are the most widely enjoyed kissing locations: top of the head ❤ forehead ❤ temples ❤ eyelids ❤ tip of the nose ❤ lips ❤ corners of the mouth ❤ chin ❤ cheeks ❤ back of neck (clavicle) ❤ shoulders ❤ shoulder blades ❤ down the backbone ❤ hollow of the neck ❤ on the ears ❤ earlobes ❤ in the hollow behind the earlobes ❤ fingertips ❤ palms ❤ toes ❤ inside surface of the arm ❤ underarm ❤ above the upper lip and below the tip of the nose ❤ eyebrows ❤ wrists ❤ inner elbow ❤ hollow of the knees ❤ breast bone ❤ arches of the feet ❤ side of the neck

KISSING EMBRACES

♥

Kissing, by design, arouses a natural desire for more body contact with your partner, and fortunately, there are many ways to arrange your body parts for kissing. (In an effort to keep these descriptions simple and succinct, the partner who should be either taller, stronger, heavier, or the primary initiator in each embrace is cast as the man. Feel free to reverse the roles.)

WITH BOTH STANDING
Front-to-Front Embraces

BASIC FRONT-TO-FRONT EMBRACE This is the most common kissing embrace. Standing in front of his partner, he places his hands on her waist. She places her hands on his waist and tilts her head backwards. Hands may hold shoulders, neck, and face as well.

SANDWICH EMBRACE She stands with her back to a wall. He, standing in front, places his hands on the wall, in a playful, nonthreatening "gotcha" manner.

BEAR HUG EMBRACE With his feet on each side of hers, he locks his arms around her upper torso to hold her tightly. She wraps her arms around his waist.

STEAM PRESS EMBRACE He wraps his arms around her upper back and applies light pressure to keep the two bodies close together. Her arms are at her side or around his neck. It is popular for the man to lift the woman off her feet.

HOOK EMBRACE She passes her hands under his arms, and then reaches up to grab the back of his shoulders. He wraps his arms around her waist.

DANCER EMBRACE Standing face to face, he holds her right hand in his left, and encircles her waist with his right arm. She rests her left hand on his right shoulder.

DIRTY DANCER EMBRACE Same body position as the "Dancer," except her left hand and his right hand relocate to other's derriere.

DIRTIER DANCER EMBRACE Both hands of each partner rest on both cheeks of their partner's derriere.

CHASTE EMBRACE Standing approximately 12 inches apart, holding hands, both lean forward to kiss.

HANGER EMBRACE With her body and face tilted considerably backward, she wraps her arms around his neck and lightly hangs while he holds on to her upper arms. This embrace will feel awkward unless the man is noticeably taller than the woman.

Front-to-Back Embraces

BASIC FRONT-TO-BACK EMBRACE He stands behind her and wraps his arms around her waist. Popular embrace for surprising or distracting your partner. Also used when waiting in line. The following three embraces are variations on this stance.

NECKTIE EMBRACE She arches backward and stretches her arms above and slightly behind her head, and wraps them around his neck.

CRADLE EMBRACE She leans backward, rests her head on his shoulder, and reaches back to put her hands in his rear pants pockets.

SIDE WINDER EMBRACE She stands behind him with her hands on his waist. She then leans to one side, nudges her head under his arm and then up to his face for a kiss.

Side-by-Side Embrace

BASIC BUDDY EMBRACE Standing shoulder to shoulder, you encircle your partner with the arm closest to his or her waist. Popular for walking together. Other hand positions are on necks or shoulders.

WITH ONE STANDING, THE OTHER SITTING

NOTE: The impact of the following embraces will vary with the choice of sitting object (chair, stool, counter, bed).

Front-to-Front Embraces

WRAPPER EMBRACE The seated woman wraps her legs around the legs of her standing partner, encircles his waist with her arms, and tilts her head back.

CORNER POCKET EMBRACE He sits with his legs parted. She stands between his legs and holds onto him around his neck. He holds onto her waist.

CAGE EMBRACE The standing man leans forward and places his hands on the arms of her chair. She, keeping her hands in her lap, tilts her head back to receive the kiss.

Front-to-Back Embraces

BEND AND STRETCH EMBRACE The seated woman stretches her head back, while the man behind bends forward. His hands rest on her shoulders.

HARNESS EMBRACE He leans over the seated woman and wraps his arms loosely around her neck.

RUB-DOWN EMBRACE Standing behind her, he runs his hands down the woman's arms and leans forward to give her a kiss. She reaches back with her hands to run them down his legs.

SITTING ON THE OTHER'S LAP

BASIC LAP EMBRACE   Sitting with her legs across his lap, she wraps her arms around his neck. His arms rest around her waist. She may also hold his hand.

LAP CRADLE   She sits on his left knee and leans into his left shoulder. His left hand is placed around her shoulders, his right hand on her cheek.

SURPRISE DUNK EMBRACE   With her sitting across his lap, he unexpectedly spreads his legs.

LAP STACK EMBRACE   Sitting on his lap as if it were a chair, she leans backward and lays her head on one of his shoulders. His arms come forward to wrap around her waist. There are two variations on this: (1) his arms rest around her shoulders and her hands come up to rest on his arms; (2) he places his hands on her legs, and she places her hands on top of his hands.

LAP STRADDLE EMBRACE   Straddling his lap, she wraps her arms around his neck. He holds on to her by wrapping his arms around her waist.

COUCH EMBRACES

BASIC COUCH POTATO EMBRACE   He reclines with the back of his head in her lap. She, seated, rests one arm on his chest, the other arm at her side, under his head or holding his free hand.

BACK-AGAINST-THE-COUCH EMBRACE   Sitting on the floor with his back resting against the couch, he parts and bends his legs. She sits between his legs and leans back against his chest. Her hands rest on the top of his bent legs. His arms encircle her waist.

SPORTS POTATO EMBRACE   Any embrace that allows him to kiss while keeping one eye on the score. One arm must always be free to express "high 5" gestures or to operate the remote controller.

COUCH À LA CARTE EMBRACE   Any couch embrace that enables one partner to reach the food on the coffee table.

ANTI-VOYEUR EMBRACE   Any couch embrace that hides the two of you from nearby siblings, roommates, or parents.

WITH BOTH RECLINING
Stack Embraces

BASIC STACK EMBRACE   She, lying face down on top of him, puts her hands under his head or shoulders. He wraps his arms around her body. (This is a good position when kissing is going to last a while.)

ROLLER EMBRACE   Basic stack embrace with the partners taking turns on top by rolling to one side.

FROG EMBRACE   Woman on top has her legs in the frog position.

SPREAD EAGLE EMBRACE   He lies on the floor face up with his arms spread and legs slightly parted. She lies on top of the man face down and mirrors his position.

BASIC RECLINING-ON-YOUR-SIDE EMBRACE   Both lie on their side, and face one another. Her arm closest to the ground wraps around his neck. Her other arm wraps around his shoulders. His closest arm to the ground goes just under her arm. His top arm wraps around her waist. Designed to have as much body surface touching the other as possible. (Warning: arms may fall alseep if not in the proper locations.)

CATAMARAN EMBRACE   Both lying face down, each's head turns toward one another. Closest arm around the other. (Also called the kissamaran.)

EMBRACES FOR EVERY OCCASION

THRESHOLD EMBRACE He holds her in his arms as if she were his bride and carries her across the threshold.

YING AND YANG EMBRACE Each lies on his or her side in a semi-fetus position. The two hook together at the lips from opposite directions.

BRIDGE EMBRACE Both lying head-to-head on their stomachs on the floor. Each arches up on his or her elbows and holds the other's hands.

CASANOVA EMBRACE Standing profile to her partner, she leans back onto his outstretched left arm. While she holds on to his lower right arm, he further tilts back her face with his right hand to plant a kiss on her upturned lips.

CAROUSEL EMBRACE With the two of you in a standing embrace, rotate clockwise or counterclockwise as you kiss. Some like to simulate a carousel and bob up and down as they circle.

TWIRL EMBRACE She grasps his neck with her arms. He takes her by the waist and lifts her off her feet. He then twirls around in a circle and the two exchange a long kiss.

"GOTCHA" EMBRACE The woman lies on her back with her hands above her head. The man sits on her waist and playfully holds her wrists with his hands as if to pin her down.

KAYAK EMBRACE The woman sits behind her partner with her legs outside of his. The upper part of her body leans forward to be in close contact with his back. She wraps her arms tightly around his waist. Kisses are placed principally along the back of his neck and the sides of his face. Variations on this embrace included: (1) she pokes her head under one of his arms to be kissed on the face; (2) she wraps her legs around his waist, and her arms encircle his chest; (3) he leans his head back to rest on one of her shoulders, making it possible for her to kiss his cheek and mouth.

❤

A FINAL WORD

❤

Human beings were meant to kiss; we are perfectly configured for the activity. We communicate standing upright, face to face and eye to eye. Our lips protrude, our tongues extend, our heads gyrate, and our arms embrace. The only possible addition might have been a tail to wag in delight.

Kissing is an art. It should be constantly refined and never neglected. Kissing is also the most intimate method we have for communicating with our partner. It ripens our emotional and physical understanding of each other, and it fuels intimacy.

My goal has been to open your minds to the endless possibilities of kissing, make you aware of the kissing techniques that get the best responses, and help you become a better kisser. I also hope you have been enlightened and amused to the point that you can't wait to find a partner to experiment on.